The Thong Principle

The Thong Principle

Saying What You Mean and Meaning What You Say

donalee Moulton

The Thong Principle: Saying What You Mean and Meaning What You Say

Copyright © Business Expert Press, LLC, 2022.

Cover design by Rand Gaynor

Interior design by Exeter Premedia Services Private Ltd., Chennai, India

All rights reserved. No part of this publication may be reproduced, stored in a retrieval system, or transmitted in any form or by any means—electronic, mechanical, photocopy, recording, or any other except for brief quotations, not to exceed 400 words, without the prior permission of the publisher.

First published in 2022 by
Business Expert Press, LLC
222 East 46th Street, New York, NY 10017
www.businessexpertpress.com

ISBN-13: 978-1-63742-210-6 (paperback)
ISBN-13: 978-1-63742-211-3 (e-book)

Business Expert Press Corporate Communication Collection

First edition: 2022

10 9 8 7 6 5 4 3 2 1

To my best friend, my mother Myrtle Moulton 1928–2020

Description

***The Thong Principle* has little to do with beachwear and everything to do with effective communication.** It's about ensuring messages are successful for the sender—and the receiver.

The book delves into the elements that comprise successful communications—conciseness, clarity, concreteness, and much more. It also puts those elements into context. Communications that miss the mark confuse and annoy. They fail to deliver their message. They damage our credibility and erode goodwill.

The Thong Principle overflows with **real-world examples** to help us understand why we fail to get our messages across as intended.

Then it explains how we can **anticipate, identify, and correct errors and oversights**. This is both at the highest level—including building and maintaining trust—and down in the weeds where even one word makes a difference.

The Thong Principle will draw you in and keep you reading with:

- Examples
- Exercises
- Information that resonates.

It's also funny. *Laughter and learning are wonderful partners.*

Keywords

communications; written communications; presentations; plain language; conciseness; feedback; editing; tone; trust; goodwill; elevated language; readability; reading ease; readability score; readability formula; proofreading; clarity; revising; thong; spinach

Contents

Testimonials xi
Acknowledgments xiii
Introduction xv

Chapter 1   Speak Your ~~Veracity~~ Truth—and Their ~~Vernacular~~ Language 1
Chapter 2   Come Again? 7
Chapter 3   Saying What You Mean in as Few Words as Possible Without Going on and on and on Unnecessarily and Including Information That Is Not Relevant and More Stuff 17
Chapter 4   Substance Abuse 33
Chapter 5   It's Not What You Say, It's How You Say It, Idiot 47
Chapter 6   Trust Me: This Is Fundamental 57
Chapter 7   Plain Language—Who Gives a Crap 73
Chapter 8   Revising, Reworking, Revitalizing 91
Chapter 9   Proofredding 105
Chapter 10   To Give and Receive 113

About the Author 123
Index 125

Testimonials

"In her new book, The Thong Principle: Saying What You Mean and Meaning What You Say, donalee Moulton delivers an informative, practical, and humorous guide to communicating effectively. Drawing on three decades of experience, donalee identifies common issues and proposes solutions, not the least of which is the need to demonstrate authenticity. 'While you want to look and sound good when you share information and insights, you also want to look and sound like yourself,' writes donalee. It is this focus on authenticity, she argues, that is the very underpinning of getting across a message. 'Listeners and readers are looking to connect with a human being. If you don't sound like one, they can't connect with you. If they can't connect with you, they won't trust you.'

Using your authentic self to build a relationship with an audience is exactly how donalee engages with hers. Anyone who has ever had an opportunity to attend a workshop or just sip coffee with this author will immediately recognize her wit, irreverent charm, and ability to get right to the point. Readers will appreciate donalee's straight talk and the book's theme: listeners and readers should not be tasked with deciphering messages. The responsibility to communicate clearly falls on the shoulders of the person or persons who have something they need and want to say. If you are one of those people, this book should be high on your reading list."—**Clare O'Connor, Principal, Full Picture Public Affairs Inc.**

"Having this book in hand is almost as good as having donalee in person. The Plain Language training she provided for our staff got rave reviews and, most importantly, results. People learned skills they were able to immediately put into practice. It became clear during the workshops, as in this book, that she is an expert in her field. She really knows her stuff! A must read for anyone who wants to communicate clearly."—**Lynn Bruce, Marketing & Outreach Officer, Vermont Department for Children and Families** "donalee has been my go-to authority on clear, concise and effective writing for over three decades. In this easy-to-read, practical and entertaining guide to 'saying what you mean and meaning what you say,' she uses wit and wisdom to tackle the challenging and technical aspects of effective writing. This is a must-read for everyone from novice to professional on how to communicate with precision and impact."—**Cathy Jacob, Writer, Leadership Coach, Cofounder of Fire Inside Leadership Inc.**

"This book is irreverent, as the title suggests. But it's steeped in respect—respect for clear communication and for your audience. If you cling to the notion that communication should be lofty and full of jargon or officialese, this book is your permission to let go. It's your safety net too, giving you the tools you need to start writing clearly and concisely.

Here, you'll learn what 'plain language' really means, and that it isn't just a good idea—it's often the law! You'll learn how to start using it. Professional communicator donalee Moulton has packed this book with real-life examples. They show that clear messaging, thoughtfully crafted and carefully checked, can not only save you from embarrassment; it can also save money, and can even save lives."—**Sue MacLeod, Certified Professional Editor**

Acknowledgments

You are reading this book because many people—family, friends, colleagues—have offered their support, insight, time to make it a reality. I owe them a debt of gratitude.

I would like to thank Cheryl Enman, my friend and co-worker, for reading, rereading, then reading once again various drafts of this book. It is thanks to Cheryl's skill with word processing and other software programs that formatting and illustrations are consistent and clear. She was also willing to accept that when it comes to commas, there is no common ground.

My appreciation also goes out to Rand Gaynor and Catherine Harrop, friends and colleagues, who served as readers for this book before it was submitted to the publisher. Working willingly under a tight deadline, they provided thoughtful, detailed, and gentle feedback that made the book better.

On a personal note, I would like to thank my husband, Allan Kindervater, for his continued patience and support. I have an ongoing attachment to my laptop and a lifetime love of language, both of which can often get in the way of daily routines and plans. He has never complained. Indeed, he has encouraged me to pursue my passions. Always.

I have been blessed to have lifelong support from my parents, Fred and Myrtle Moulton. My mother taught me at an early age about the wonder and joy of words that I still savor today. Both my parents made it clear, without ever having to use words, that whatever I wanted to do with my life had their full, utter, and complete blessing. Such unconditional support is the foundation for a life full of wonder. And words.

Introduction

What's in a Name

In the case of this book, everything.

The Thong Principle is a way of communicating and a way of thinking. It's about, as the subtitle indicates, a way to communicate that works on all levels. A way of communicating that works for the person sending the message and the person or people receiving the message.

As participants who've taken my courses know, I've been talking about the Thong Principle for decades. It's a way to remember what matters most when we're trying to convey a message. It's a reminder that how we convey a message is as important as what we have to say.

The name came to me after spending several glorious days on a beach in Mexico (or it may have been the Dominican Republic). One thing is certain, the sand was white, the ocean aquamarine, and the skies ablaze with sun.

Under the rules of this particular resort, cabanas could only be reserved on a first-come, first-served basis. A kind fellow who was part of our group got up every morning at five o'clock (bless his heart) and staked out prime territory for us on the beach. The rest of us awoke to find our towels, chairs, and beach hut ready and waiting. Here we would spend the day until dinner called us in for the evening.

As you sit under a dried palm umbrella, icy marguerita within easy reach, and a best-selling mystery novel in hand, there is little to do but enjoy life, fill your lungs with gratitude, and look up every once in a while to soak in the atmosphere. As I looked up, and walked the beach, it occurred to me that many vacationers were wearing thongs. Yep, the swimsuit with a single string in the rear.

Admittedly, many of them looked good, very good. Of course, when you see enough people opting to wear an outfit with less material than my cat's harness, it raises a very personal question: Should I wear a thong?

After of week of looking and lounging, I had my answer. *No.*

Whatever carefree attitude, chutzpah, confidence, or complacency it took to walk up and down a public beach with your ass hanging out, I didn't have it. (Still don't.) Initially, that realization surprised me and disappointed me. I wanted to be the lighthearted beach walker who meandered blithely up and down the sand without a care in the world about my bare ass, who was looking, or how I ranked on the thong-wearing scale.

I came to realize, however, that my reluctance to wear a thong was just that. Mine. It's about comfort, physically and emotionally. I am not a thong wearer. I've learned to live with that.

I've also come to realize this reality is the foundation of effective communication. While you want to look good and sound good when you share information and insights, you also want to look and sound like yourself. Indeed, it's essential that you do. Anything else will sound forced, unnatural, and suspicious. It will raise two questions: Do you know what you're talking about? Are you being honest with me?

And that's the thong principle. Rely on the material in this and other documents to help you understand the essential elements of effective communication, but understand ultimately, it's about trust. Your reader or your listener has to trust you do know what you're talking about. They have to trust you're being upfront with them. If they don't, whatever you have to say will fail to resonate. In fact, you may end up sending a message you never intended to send.

The thong principle isn't about appearances. It's about getting your message across in the way you intended with the information you intended actually being understood. Otherwise, why bother.

You might as well stay inside the resort and order room service.

CHAPTER 1

Speak Your ~~Veracity~~ Truth—and Their ~~Vernacular~~ Language

Participants in many of the classes I teach and many of the clients I work with tell me—apologetically—"I write like I speak." It's offered up as an explanation as to why their written communication often fails. In fact, the reverse is true.

Listeners and readers are looking to connect with a human being. If you don't sound like one, they can't connect with you. If they can't connect with you, they won't trust you. And the circle of miscommunication is complete.

We've gotten it into our heads and our hearts since elementary school teachers graded our first essay and announced we would have to give a "presentation," that communicating professionally was somehow different from all the other types of communicating we do: having a heartfelt conversation with our best friend, talking to the grocery store clerk as they scan our items through the checkout, greeting a colleague in the lunchroom after a long weekend. Yet the people we talk with—in writing, in person, via Zoom, over the phone—tell us otherwise.

One particularly irksome culprit that gets in the way of clear communication is elevated language. This is us getting dressed for the Oscars when all that's really required are comfortable slacks and a clean shirt.

So why do we communicate in a language that isn't natural to us?

Two Reasons.
First. We often feel like we're not impressing people with our knowledge, our skills, and our insight when we use everyday language. It's too ordinary, and we want our subject or ourselves (or both) to stand out. Using language that isn't plain will indeed make us stand out, but not in the way we intended or the way we want.

Second. We've been trained to write and speak like a dictionary wedded to a thesaurus. Once we hit junior high, then high school, then university, we were rewarded for our use of big words, long sentences, and repetitive thoughts. Fair enough. But this is an academic environment where pushing ourselves and our ideas is paramount. When we exit the hallowed halls of academia and enter the real world, the rules change. Our bosses, our customers, our coworkers aren't looking for us to use words they have to ask Siri to look up or take 40 pages to tell us what could be said in 10. Frankly, it wastes their time, and it's frustrating.

So what's wrong if we use fancy words people aren't familiar with?

Two Things.
Content. When we use words people don't instantly and naturally understand, we open the door to miscommunication. Now we all think we're bright (because we are), but the reality is that language is specialized and becoming more so. The language we use when we're having lunch with a friend or picking out a puppy at the shelter is the language that comes most naturally to us. It's also the language that is most easily and instantly understood by the person we're communicating with.

Let me give you a famous example. When entrepreneur P.T. Barnum opened Barnum's American Museum in New York 180 years ago, he wanted it to become one of the greatest attractions in the country. And he succeeded. Between 1841 and 1865, roughly 38 million customers forked over a quarter to set foot inside the museum. At that time, there were only 32 million people in America.

So volume was critical to Barnum's success. It didn't take long for the wily museum owner to realize that moving people through the exhibits

SPEAK YOUR ~~VERACITY~~ TRUTH—AND THEIR ~~VERNACULAR~~ LANGUAGE

quickly was essential for greater profit. However, visitors wanted to linger at the flea circus, gawk at the loom powered by a dog, and admire the glass blowers.

Instead of raising the price of admission to raise more money or have exhibit staff nudge people along, Barnum did what many great marketers have done over the course of history. He fooled his customers by using a language they didn't understand.

Barnum posted a sign that read, "This Way to the Egress." Well who wouldn't want to see a magnificent egress? However, "egress" means "exit." Barnum wasn't directing people to another fabulous, outrageous, incredible display, he was literally sending them back outdoors. He knew if the sign read "exit" people would go in another direction. He knew if he used a term they weren't familiar with, they would willingly usher themselves outdoors. One word and problem solved.

But that is short-term profit for long-term mistrust.

This Way to Comprehension

The reality is this. When we use a language our audience doesn't understand—deliberately or inadvertently—we run a high risk they won't get our message. And that's the whole reason we communicated in the first place. If readers and listeners don't understand what we're saying to them, we won't achieve our purpose; indeed, we may achieve the opposite of what we intended, and it's likely we'll have to communicate again. That wastes everyone's time—and impresses no one.

Well, we could argue that if our readers don't understand the language we're using, they should look it up. Indeed, they could. But we know this: The longer it takes for someone to get our message, the more difficult we make it, the more work that is involved, the less likely they are to finish reading or listening, and the more annoyed they'll become. Our job is to make our communication as simple and straightforward as possible so we can accomplish our purpose.

We also have to be realistic about our own language. We are intelligent, we are educated, we are articulate, yet our day-to-day conversation comes in at a Grade 8 level or lower, which we'll talk more about in the plain language chapter. Speaking simply and clearly is the most efficient and effective way to get things done, to ensure our message is interpreted as intended, and to build that all-important trust with our audience.

Frankly, specialized and elevated language is not easily understood by most of us. That reality was tragically underscored on January 28, 1986, when the space shuttle Challenger exploded 73 seconds after its launch. All seven crew members were killed. A subsequent review of the disaster included a close examination of a memo issued before the shuttle launch that warned a critical O-ring might not work—with lethal results.

Unfortunately, that warning was not clear to readers. The dire consequences were identified only after a long, wordy, jargon-filled introduction and even then, the warning was not heralded clearly. The tone and the words did not impact urgency or make it immediately clear the launch was in imminent danger.

Here's some of what was said.

> Bench test data indicate that the O-ring resiliency (its capability to follow the metal) is a function of temperature and rate of case expansion. MTI measured the force of the O-ring against Instron patters, which simulated the nominal squeeze on the O-ring and approximated the case expansion distance and rate.
>
> At 100 degrees F., the O-ring maintained contact. At 75 degrees F., the O-ring lost contact for 2.4 seconds. At 50 degrees F., the O-ring did not re-establish contact in ten minutes at which time the test was terminated.
>
> The conclusion is that secondary sealing capability in the SRM field joint cannot be guaranteed.

Nowhere does it read, "Because of potential O-ring failure, the shuttle could be torn apart." That readers would instantly understand.

Today, NASA has committed to writing in a language easily and instantly understood by the public. This pronouncement follows the *Plain Language Act of 2010*, which requires all federal agencies to communicate clearly so that the public can understand and use the information.

Here is NASA's commitment to following that law:

SPEAK YOUR ~~VERACITY~~ TRUTH—AND THEIR ~~VERNACULAR~~ LANGUAGE

Our Promise to You: Writing You Can Understand

We at NASA are committed to writing all of our new documents in plain language that you can understand. Our goal is to use plain language in any document that:

- Is necessary for obtaining any of our benefits or services
- Provides information about any of our benefits or services
- Explains how to comply with a requirement that we administer or enforce

But what if my audience does understand my highfalutin language?

What is easily understood by everyone is the language of conversation. Now if that conversation is between two cardiologists, the use of "myocardial infarction" makes perfect sense. If the heart specialists are speaking with a patient, however, the preferable term would be "heart attack." Not only would this mean something to the patient, it would make them feel part of the conversation.

It can be difficult to let go of the belief that straightforward language is less effective—and less impressive. But we all know the sinking feeling when the expert or the office showoff gets up to make a presentation or we walk into our office on a Monday morning to see that some thoughtful soul has left a 40-page report on our desk. There is an immediate and instinctive response. It's not pleasant.

Our first thought is that this thick tome is going to be dry. It's going to be dull. It's going to be repetitive. And it's going to be written in a language we don't understand. Who wants that? No one.

Length is linked to writing and speaking that encourages readers and listeners to tune out rather than dive in. In part, that has to do with content. We're afraid we're not going to easily understand what is being said. We'll have to have a dictionary and a thesaurus close at hand.

But it's also about being part of the communication. Jargon, the myocardial infarction crew, has its place. It says to your audience, "We share a special language." However, when you use that language—or any language readers don't readily understand, you send the message that your audience is not part of the inner circle. They don't belong here.

How does it make you feel to be left out?

We call that communication that excludes. If you want your reader or listener to continue, you need to interest and engage them. You need to make them feel included. You need to speak their language. It's not about dumbing down. It's about efficiency and respect.

It's also about trust. When your audience can't determine easily what it is you're trying to say, they begin to question your motives. Did you not care about them or their issue? Do you not really understand what they need? Are you trying to hide behind this fancy language? It is this mistrust that has led to laws compelling organizations, government, and business to communicate in an instantly understandable language. It is this mistrust that has led to the plain language movement, a global call for communications that can be understood.

We think we sound great when we use more difficult and unusual language. We do the opposite. We sound stuffy, pompous, and arrogant. We come across as boring at best, deceitful at worst.

So in summary, when we use a language that is not familiar to our audience, we run the risk that they will not understand what it is we are trying to say to them. We run the risk that we will distance ourselves from readers and listeners. We'll build distrust and a disconnect.

'Nuf said.

CHAPTER 2

Come Again?

Say what you have to say—clearly

The problem with readers and listeners is (1) they aren't as bright as us and (2) they don't dwell inside our heads. We're communicating clearly, articulately, and sincerely, brilliantly even, and they're saying "Duh." Then they yawn.

To be fair, we may be partly to blame for the confusion, the ambiguity, and the lack of clarity. That's, in part, because we intuitively understand our own message, and we are usually focused on what we want to say, how we want to say it, and why it is important to us. Audiences, however, are listening to radio station WII-FM, What's In It For Me.

That sounds selfish. It isn't. We're bombarded with incoming and outgoing messages. With respect to e-mail alone, the average office employee receives about 121 e-mails a day. That doesn't include the 40 they send for work. We've adapted to the communication volume—in person, online, via telephone, and otherwise—by becoming adept at quickly and efficiently discarding those messages that are not relevant or easily understandable. Indeed, the decision to keep, read, or trash an e-mail is made in less than three seconds.

We simply don't have time to review and ponder every message, verbal or written. If you want to impress your audience, you need to give them information that is clear, concise and important—to them.

That starts by shifting the focus from you to your audience. Say, for example, you want to reach out to potential participants about an upcoming course you feel may be of interest to them. Advanced cake decorating with spinach, perhaps. Don't tell them this course is great because you have a birthday coming up and love green velvet cake. That may be accurate. But it's also irrelevant in their lives.

That is what we call writer-focused communication. You want audience-focused communication. In this case, they might be interested to know a cake decorating class can save them money, earn them oohs and aahs from family and friends, and spark their creativity.

Let's Be Clear

The You Attitude, as it is commonly called, saves words and makes sure a message is targeted to the reader or listener. That doesn't mean it will be understood. There are two key components to clarity. The first, as we've discussed, is word choice. Will your reader understand the technical terms, the jargon, the inflated language? Or will the language confuse them, bore them, and turn them off?

Take this message for instance:

A perissodactyl ungulate may be propelled toward a body of aqueous fluid, but such ungulate cannot be compelled or forcibly induced to imbibe such fluid.

It's a perfectly grammatically correct English sentence. That doesn't make it understandable. Or interesting. Or impressive. Now readers might know one or two words and from there determine what they believe the sentence is saying.

We call this guessing.

Do you really want your audience to guess at what it is you're trying to tell them? Invariably, they will guess wrong, and we will have miscommunicated. We may have to communicate again, which wastes everybody's time. Even if they guess correctly, it's luck, not design. We want to be skillful at communicating, not merely fortunate.

Instead of saying this:

A perissodactyl ungulate may be propelled toward a body of aqueous fluid, but such ungulate cannot be compelled or forcibly induced to imbibe such fluid.

We could say this:

You can lead a horse to water, but you can't make it drink.

Two things happen when we make the language conversational. First, our audience gets what it is we want them to know. Once this happens, they become informed; they make sounder decisions; they feel included in the discussion. Second, they don't think we're an idiot. In fact, they think we're quite bright. They actually read our e-mails when they arrive in the inbox; they listen when we have something to say.

Words matter. That implies you have a choice, and choices require thought. If you rush through a call or fire off a message en route to a meeting, chances are you'll miss the mark. Either the content won't be clear or the tone those words convey won't be what you intended. We'll talk about tone later. For now, let's put a little effort into making our messages understandable because the language is shared.

Yep, I Know What ya Mean

Clarity is about more than elevated language and jargon. It's about making sure the words we use convey the meaning we intended. What's crystal clear to us as the originator of the message, may in fact be open to interpretation.

Take this actual scenario. A dear friend several years ago had a crush on this guy. Let's call him Dick Wadd.

She's out walking around one noon hour and runs into Dick. They stop to chat. He tells her his folks, the Wadds, are in town and he's been taking them to all the local tourist spots. Then he says, oh joy, oh bliss, "Why don't we go out for dinner after they leave?"

My friend, trying to contain her delight and failing miserably, I'm sure, says, "When?"

Dick suggests next Friday.

So it's Wednesday. This gives my friend 10 days to drive me nuts. Should she get her nails done? Hair cut? You want to look good, but not like you're trying too hard. Then there is the question of what to wear. It will be a long 10 days for me.

A few days after Dick Wadd asks my friend out she's walking home from work when her phone rings. It's Dick, and he's obviously annoyed. "Where are you?" he asks. Tersely.

"On my way home," my friend responds.

"We have a date," DW counters.

"Next Friday," my friend says, starting to get a tinch annoyed herself. "This is next Friday," Dick says and hangs up.

Recap: When Dick Wadd suggests they get together "next" Friday, he means the very next Friday on the calendar. My friend hears "next" Friday and immediately knows he doesn't want to go out "this" Friday, so it must be the Friday after that.

It's an issue of clarity. Can the words you use be interpreted in ways you didn't intend. If Dick had said, "Let's get together this Friday," or "How about May 3rd?," there would have been only one way to interpret that message. There would have been a connection instead of a disconnect.

My friend married someone else.

Going With the Flow

Choosing your words carefully is important. Putting them in the right order—from your audience's perspective—is equally important. The right words in the wrong order will still confuse your reader or listener. This happens all the time. We say, "A, B, C, E" and your audience is left wondering what the hell happened to "D"? In our mind, it was there when we drafted the text or opened our mouth—because we know what we intended to say.

The other common problem is this. We say, "A, B, D, C," and readers are left wondering why you'd try to get the horse to drink before you led it to water. Again, because we're so familiar with what the intention of the message was, we understand it.

This is about organizing your thoughts and your information in a way that flows logically and smoothly.

Take this letter, for instance. A private company has to turn down a charity's request for signage. Here's what was written.

> We have received your request dated October 17, 2021, for approval to erect a sign in front of our parking lot, which is located on the corner of Kale Street and Confusion Avenue. We always strive to support local organizations. You are the heart of our community.

However, parking is an ongoing issue for our company. At present, there are a number of signs posted in the parking lot, and we are concerned that another sign would create misunderstanding. We must, therefore, respectfully decline your request.

On the surface, this letter sounds professional and reasonable. But let's get inside the reader's mind.

Sentence 1

We have received your request dated October 17, 2021, for approval to erect a sign in front of our parking lot, which is located on the corner of Kale Street and Confusion Avenue.

What the reader is thinking: I know why I wrote you. I know when I wrote you (or I don't care about the date). Why are you feeding me back what I already know in detail? Yawn.

Sentence 2

We always strive to support local organizations.

What the reader is thinking: Of course you do—and so modestly. Many readers will consider this little more than sucking up and patting yourself on the back. Many will also think with this sentence right up front in the message good news is about to follow. It isn't, so their disappointment will be increased.

Sentence 3

You are the heart of our community.

What the reader is thinking: You're really laying it on now. Things are definitely going my way.

Sentence 4

However, parking is an ongoing issue for our company.

What the reader is thinking: Dear God, you've misinterpreted my letter. I wasn't asking about parking. I was asking about a sign. A little panic and frustration sets in.

Now, chances are the parking problem is linked to a sign problem, as the writer well knows. Unfortunately, the reader doesn't have that insight.

Sentence 5, Part 1

At present, there are a number of signs posted in the parking lot …

What the reader is thinking: Woohoo! I'm going to get my sign posted. (Now imagine how they feel when they discover they're not going to get their sign, but others got the go-ahead.)

Sentence 5, Part 2

… and we are concerned that another sign would create misunderstanding.

What the reader is thinking: What are they going to be confused about? It's a parking lot. You pull in. You turn off the ignition. Are you concerned customers will think your company is a charity? Well, that's just stupid.

Sentence 6

We must, therefore, respectfully decline your request.

What the reader is thinking: Piss off.

What Causes a Lack of Lucidity?

Primarily it's lack of awareness. Too often we're convinced we're saying things clearly and straightforwardly even though we're not. What's crystal clear to us—because we know the topic, we understand our own language, and we know what we want to say—is not necessarily as easily understood by the audience. That's why we need to shift focus from what we want to say to what the audience needs to hear.

Let me give you an example. I was recently in a meeting with a group of trainers and the employee who oversees training for the provincial government in question. We were trying to set dates for upcoming training sessions. So you have eight people, phones out, calendars at the ready. The government's training director, a lovely and highly competent woman, suggested we try to avoid Mondays and Fridays because they are EDOs.

I stumbled over the acronym EDO. No idea what this meant. I thought to myself, "EDOs. That would be extraterrestrial dynasties overseas." Then I thought, "Well, that's just silly. EDO—Employees Designated Obnoxious." Nope, equally silly. Of course, the whole time I'm trying to decipher the meaning, I'm not paying attention to what is going on in the meeting. I'm elsewhere, and during my journey, dates have been set. Dates, naturally, that don't work for me.

If my colleague had said, "Let's avoid Mondays and Fridays because they are often earned days off for employees," I would have understood the message and kept up with the flow of the meeting. Even if she had suggested we avoid EDOs, or earned days off, I would have been able to follow along.

I wasn't alone. Several other people had also tuned out, and we all had to review our calendars and the proposed dates again. An unnecessary waste of time.

And our little group isn't unique. An article in the *Harvard Business Review* by Josh Bernoff detailed the results of a survey of 547 businesspeople who write at least two hours a week—over and above e-mail—and spend another roughly 26 hours reading material, including e-mail. More than 80 percent of respondents said poorly written material wastes a lot of their time. What makes something poorly written, they were asked? It's too long, poorly organized, unclear, filled with jargon, and open to interpretation.

Your Reputation Is on the Line

While ineffective communication is a pain for both the person receiving the message and the person sending it, the problem with unclear, wordy, disorganized communication goes beyond the message itself. Our reputation is at stake.

People form an opinion of us based on what we say and what we do. When our communication fails to hit home, readers and listeners attribute this to us not knowing how to communicate well (a lack of skill and ability) or not caring to take the time to communicate effectively (indifference or arrogance). Either way our credibility is tarnished. This is another reason why audiences don't pay attention to what we have to say. We train them not to listen because the message will be difficult or we're not worth a lot of their time. Or both.

The desire to sound educated and erudite (now, there's a word we'll need to look up) often compels us to use fancy words, long sentences, repetitive content. It's the 40-page-report syndrome. This syndrome can also affect our credibility in unintended ways. The language we use day in and day out, at work, at home, and at play, is the language of conversation. When we elevate that language, we frequently misstep and land on our asses.

Let me give you an example. A friend of mine (you met her and her prospective beau, Dick Wadd, earlier) was making a presentation to the senior executive team of a telecommunications company. My friend, let's call her Olive, is a marketing whiz. She and her team had spent months reviewing the company's existing marketing approach and its success. Then they explored how to improve on both. Significantly. Now they were bringing their proposal forward to the senior team for sign-off.

It was a big deal, and Olive worked long and hard to make sure they were given the go-ahead and the budget needed to change their marketing direction. Within minutes of the presentation ending, she was at my desk suggesting we have a coffee. Once seated, I asked how the presentation went. She said, "Well," but hesitated.

Then Olive looked at me. "I think it might have been a little over their heads."

When I asked how she had reached this conclusion, Olive asked me if I knew what this word meant, and she spelled it for me: h-y-p-e-r-b-o-l-e.

I told her I did; it meant exaggerating or overstating something. Olive nodded, smiled, then sighed. "I don't think the executive team knows what it means. They looked at me strangely when I used it."

Oh dear. "What did you say?" I asked.

"I explained," Olive said, "that our current marketing approach relied on hyberbowl."

Unfortunately, it didn't. As the executive team knew, it relied on hy-per-bo-lee.

And one last example to drive home the point. I was at an annual banquet with another friend, not Olive, who sat on the board of directors of a regional credit union. After dinner, came the speeches. Each year members who were leaving the board were thanked by the president. In this case, the president was quite new to the job, and he was sincerely thanking a long-term board member he clearly considered a mentor.

At one point, he was listing some of the member's many attributes and said, "Of course, we all enjoy his self-depreciating sense of humor."

I looked up quickly and saw several other heads look up with me. The term is "self-deprecating." I'm not sure if this was a slip of the tongue, a little bit of humor ("depreciating" is a banking-related word for diminishing), or if the president didn't know the correct word.

That was several years ago. I can't remember the name of the credit union, or the president, or the person leaving the board. But I can remember the error.

I'm not alone.

By the Numbers

- According to a 2019 article in the *Harvard Business Review*, the average professional spends 28 percent of the workday reading and answering emails. For the average full-time worker in the United States, that amounts to 2.6 hours a day.
- A survey of more than 1,000 Americans conducted by Adobe Inc., found this number was almost twice as high: workers said they spent 5 hours a day reading e-mail.

Decipher This

Original (from the U.K. Plain English Campaign)

Your enquiry about the use of the entrance area at the library for the purpose of displaying posters and leaflets about Welfare and Supplementary Benefit rights, gives rise to the question of the provenance and authoritativeness of the material to be displayed. Posters and leaflets issued by the Central Office of Information, the Department of Health and Social Security and other authoritative bodies are usually displayed in libraries, but items of a disputatious or polemic kind, whilst not necessarily excluded, are considered individually.

Rewritten

Thank you for your letter asking for permission to put up posters in the library. Before we can give you an answer we will need to see a copy of the posters to make sure they won't offend anyone.

CHAPTER 3

Saying What You Mean in as Few Words as Possible Without Going on and on and on Unnecessarily and Including Information That Is Not Relevant and More Stuff

Conciseness is Critical

This chapter is about saying what you mean without adding unnecessary details, words, or ideas. In short, it's about conciseness.

The first step en route to writing and speaking concisely is understanding what's meant by conciseness. The shortest government e-mail, the briefest Oscar acceptance speech, and the thinnest committee report all might, in fact, be wordy. Conciseness does not mean shortest, it means the shortest possible communication that is still complete.

So, briefly, let's look at why conciseness is important.

Omitting information will only raise questions or lead to poor decision making. Taking out facts, qualifiers, and important context means your audience may lose the thread of what you're saying and lose interest. Or become increasingly confused.

Conciseness is also linked to tone. Sometimes we add words to soften what we're saying and to give readers and listeners time to absorb our message. Indeed, longer sentences are generally softer sentences. Adding words for this purpose isn't being verbose. It's being smart.

Now let's look at why conciseness is an issue.

There are three steps to communicating, a reality that surprises many people. The first step is preparing, getting ready to speak or write. Making sure you have all the information you need, you've thought your message through, you understand your purpose. Next, for writers and presenters, comes drafting. Putting your thoughts down so you'll be confident they flow smoothly, they make sense, they engage the audience.

Many communicators stop here. This is especially true for shorter presentations and pieces of writing. We're in a hurry, we're a professional, we know what we're talking about. We don't need to take a second look.

Yep, you do.

The final step in the communications process is editing. Looking at what you have to say and seeing how it could be said better. Conciseness plays a role here. Could words, sentences, paragraphs, examples, slides, anecdotes be shorter without losing important information or context? The answer, invariably, is yes.

It's the old adage, think before you speak. Sometimes all it takes is a deep breath to mentally revise what you were about to say. Sometimes all it takes is a quick stretch and a second glance at that e-mail to realize you forgot to ask a question or have over-explained your request.

Finally, let's look at why long-winded speakers
and lengthy documents drive us nuts.

Length irks readers and listeners for a number of reasons. And we'll get to them. First though, picture this. It's Monday morning. You've had a great weekend—friends came over, you went for a hike, the baby slept in until 5 a.m.—but now it's back to the office. You have two meetings scheduled for this morning and at least one deadline looming. And that's before you've ordered your coffee from the drive-through.

You hustle in your office and peeking out from the corner of your desk chair is a document. You pick it up. It's 40 pages long.

What's your reaction?

Almost without fail, your heart will plummet, your blood pressure will rise, your stomach will churn, and whatever optimistic outlook you had for the day will disappear. All this and you haven't even read the report yet (it could be riveting). Indeed, you haven't even glanced at the title. Your physiological reaction is based simply on the sheer length of the document. It's the same way when your boss schedules a two-hour meeting to discuss the holiday party or the 60-minute agenda calls for a 40-minute presentation on the new payroll software.

Several years ago I was asked to give a presentation to students at an elementary/junior high school. It was Writers' Week, and in addition to the poets, the novelists, and the playwrights, I was asked to speak about life as a professional writer, someone who earned their living putting words to work. The audience was tweens, kids between 9 and 12 years of age.

The talks were all being held in the school library, and while we were waiting for the thud of pre-teen footsteps, the librarian took me on a tour. The library was quite new and reflected the new way of thinking about libraries—as places to spark imagination and engagement not enforce a cone of silence. The librarian had only been in her role for a few years. She told me that as a library school student she had been given a list of criteria to use when selecting material for tweens. On that list were things like this: the main character had to overcome an obstacle; all loose ends had to be tied up; good had to win out over evil.

What wasn't on that list the librarian told me was the number one criteria for selecting material for tweens. This she learned when she left school and entered the "real world." All the other criteria she was taught at university were still important, they just weren't the most important.

So what do you think is the most important criteria for selecting a book for tweens?

Many people think it is the cover. *Nope.*

Some think it's the title? *Nope.*

It's the size of the book. Demonstrating with her hands and a great deal of laughter, the school librarian showed me what happens when a tween mistakenly pulls a large tome from a library shelf. They immediately put it back and breathe a sigh of relief. It's like they're saying, "Phew. That was close."

At the point the kids shove the book back on a shelf, they haven't glanced at the title, checked out the cover, or browsed the flip side of the book. Yet every fiber in their body is telling them to get rid of this—and quickly.

Now Harry Potter and friends may be helping to transform this almost involuntary response, but the key for us as communicators is to understand why it happens in the first place. Why you have a similar reaction when you pick up a 40-page report.

Experience has taught us to dread length. Long documents, long speeches, long meetings usually mean two things: boredom and confusion. We've been trained that lengthy documents and diatribes are synonymous with repetition, with irrelevant information, with clichés. We've come to learn that the thicker the tome the more likely we are to be faced with language we don't understand—jargon, acronyms, fancified words—and don't care about. We get left behind. We get confused. We yawn.

And we've learned this by the time we are nine.

So why would we continue to write long or speak at length?

Two reasons. First, we think we're impressing the bejesus out of people when we go on at length. We think we're showing readers and listeners how bright we are, how diligent we are, how hard we have worked. Writers believe that when people pick-up their 40-page report they will say, "Wow. Forty pages. This is impressive. This person should be promoted."

In fact, what we actually say before we've even read the report is this: "Good grief. Who's the idiot that thinks I've got time to read 40 pages."

The second reason we write long and often speak at length is because we don't edit what we're saying. We've already touched on this, but many of us stop when we've finished the first draft of our document or our presentation. We breathe a sigh of relief. "Glad that's done."

But it isn't. In fact, the work is only just starting—and it is work. Renowned humorist and author Mark Twain once said, "I didn't have time to write a short letter, so I wrote a long one instead."

Editing requires us to rethink, reorganize, and reword, but the results are well worth the effort. See for yourself in these examples from the Plain Language Action and Information Network (PLAIN), a working group of U.S. federal employees from different agencies and specialties who support the use of clear communication in government writing.

> ## Try Your Hand
>
> What would you do to make these paragraphs from the Plain Language Action and Information Network website less wordy?
>
> 1. If the State Secretary finds that an individual has received a payment to which the individual was not entitled, whether or not the payment was due to the individual's fault or misrepresentation, the individual shall be liable to repay to State the total sum of the payment to which the individual was not entitled. (54 words)
> 2. When the process of freeing a vehicle that has been stuck results in ruts or holes, the operator will fill the rut or hole created by such activity before removing the vehicle from the immediate area. (36 words)
> 3. This is a multipurpose passenger vehicle which will handle and maneuver differently from an ordinary passenger car, in driving conditions which may occur on streets and highways and off road. As with other vehicles of this type, if you make sharp turns or abrupt maneuvers, the vehicle may roll over or may go out of control and crash. You should read driving guidelines and instructions in the Owner's Manual, and WEAR YOUR SEAT BELTS AT ALL TIMES. (77 words)
>
> Turn to page 30 to see what the government departments and agencies actually did.

So what's a wordy bird to do?
Lots.

Avoid the tired and trite

We understand the elements that contribute to a lack of conciseness. Let's start with the obvious, and maybe the easiest. Some of these have to do with the words and expressions we use. Many are simply longer than they need to be.

For example what is the difference between:

In order to versus *To*
Whether or not versus *Whether*

Compare these sentences:

In order to understand why kale is inferior to spinach, we need to start with the soil.
To understand why kale is inferior to spinach, we need to start with the soil.
It's your decision whether or not you attend the meeting.
It's your decision whether you attend the meeting.

There is no difference between the comparable sentences except length. If we use "to" instead of "in order to" we reduce the number of words from three to one, or 66 percent. The same is true of "whether" versus "whether or not." It's a small thing, but if we can effectively trim documents by a third it will enhance readability and improve clarity.

There are also expressions we tend to use almost by rote. We start conversations, meetings, e-mails with familiar phrases. It's like taking the same route home every day from the office. Sometimes we pull into our driveway, not really aware how we got here. Communicating on autopilot is always risky.

These common phrases are often overused expressions or cliches. They really fall into two camps: those that have been around for decades if not centuries and those that are newer and have taken hold in the language. Here are a few examples:

> As per our conversation
> I look forward to hearing from you
> Please note that
> At the end of the day
> Win–win situation
> Think outside the box
> Let's touch base

Now these overused expressions are not likely to be misunderstood, but they are, quite simply, tired and trite. They lack impact. At the very least, they sound mundane and boring. At worst, they make us as communicators look unimaginative and half-hearted. They also add unnecessary words to our communication. Cut them out and we'll cut down on length and zero in on relevant information. Count on it.

Take action

It's also recommended—wisely—that we use the active voice. It not only requires fewer words, it's more interesting, straightforward, and easily understood. Most sentences in the English language follow an active format: subject, verb, object. Yet, many reports, policies, research papers, formal presentations, and study findings are written in the passive, not the active, voice.

Like this:

Popeye loves spinach. *Subject. Verb. Object.*

And like this in a more complex sentence:

Popeye believes spinach—not kale—is the perfect food. He thinks kale sucks. *Popeye still leads the charge.*

So let's go passively into those good sentences.

Spinach is loved by Popeye. *Object. Verb. Subject.*

The perfect food is believed by Popeye to be spinach—not kale. It is thought by Popeye that kale sucks. *Notice the "by" and "be." These are indicators the passive voice is being used.*

While we might agree with Popeye about kale, the passive voice construction is often awkward and always wordy. There are times when the passive voice is a good choice: when we want the focus on the object not the subject.
Maybe like this:

The divorce papers were signed by Brad and Angelina, who then embraced passionately.
Grammar books would tell us the important thing here is the divorce papers, not Brad and Angelina. Yeah, right.

How about this:

A great deal of meaning is conveyed by a few well-chosen words. [Passive] And a longing glance. [Not a sentence] Just ask Brad and Angelina. [Active]

Avoid repetition, repetition, repetition

As communicators we also have a tendency to repeat words, phrases, ideas, and examples. In some cases, this is done sparingly for emphasis or as a reminder of key points and messaging. Most of the time, however, it's done because we haven't taken the time to edit our writing or ourselves. Most repetition is, quite frankly, boring. It's also unnecessary. If we've shared information with our audience once, why are we telling them again. If we've used the word "situation" once in a paragraph or statement, why are we using it two additional times. (Believe me, they got the message. "There is a situation.")

Part of this issue relates to organization. If a presentation or piece of writing isn't well organized, we may have to repeat content to ensure understanding. So making sure our thoughts and content are organized logically is important. Outlines, rereading, and reading a draft out loud will all help here.

The other reason we repeat information is we haven't taken the time to edit what we've drafted in the first place. This is especially true if the talk or message is short. We think we're fine because there aren't too many words. However, editing is essential regardless of the nature of the communication, the complexity of the content, or the number of sentences/paragraphs/minutes.

In Short

Numerous other techniques can help us reduce length. Purdue University's online writing lab recommends several tips starting with replacing vague words with more powerful and specific words. Like this:

Wordy: The politician talked *about several of the merits of* after-school programs in his speech. (14 words)

Concise: The politician *touted* after-school programs in his speech.

The Purdue OWL (online writing lab) also suggests checking every word to make sure it contributes something important and unique to a sentence. If words are dead weight, they can be deleted or replaced. As in this example from the OWL website:

Wordy: Eric Clapton and Steve Winwood formed a new band of musicians together in 1969, giving it the ironic name of Blind Faith because early speculation that was spreading everywhere about the band suggested that the new musical group would be good enough to rival the earlier bands that both men had been in, Cream and Traffic, which people had really liked and had been very popular. (66 words)

Concise: Eric Clapton and Steve Winwood formed a new band in 1969, ironically naming it Blind Faith, because speculation suggested that the group would rival the musicians' previous popular bands, Cream and Traffic. (32 words)

Rely on relevance

In addition to wordsmithing, there is one other significant element to consider when looking to make sure what we say and what we write is concise: relevance. All too often we add details, describe things, and provide examples that are simply not necessary. They bore the audience (and may confuse them) and weigh our writing or presentation down.

I have a dear friend who overshares. The result is many of us tune out. I once asked her how her mother's name was placed on a waiting list for a nursing home. My friend spent 10 minutes explaining about the local health authority's home care program. I thought she had misunderstood and interjected that I was inquiring about the nursing home. My friend corrected me gently. First, she would tell me about the home care program, then nursing home care.

In her mind there was a logical connection between the two, and she had lived through both experiences. Unfortunately, I wasn't interested in the home care information. My question was about nursing home care, and I hate to admit it, but I stopped listening with any intent early into the home care explanation.

Just because something is relevant to us or interesting to us doesn't mean it will be to those we are communicating with. Indeed, remember the radio station our audience listens to avidly: WII-FM. What's In It For Me? If our audience can't find what they need in what we have to say and can't easily see how our information is relevant to them, they will simply stop paying attention. And the purpose we had for communicating will not be achieved. We will have wasted our time and theirs.

Frankly, people are fed up with colleagues, supervisors, employees, suppliers, and everyone else in their workplace wasting their time with communication that doesn't do the job it was intended to do. According to *The State of Business Writing, 2016,* 81 percent of people who write for work agree with the statement "Poorly written material wastes my time."

Leaving the listener out of the conversation or the reader out of the material is a sure-fire way to get them to stop paying attention or to half pay attention. We want their whole attention. We need to look carefully at what we're saying and ask:

- Does the audience need this information to understand what I'm saying or asking of them?
- Does the audience already know this information?
- Does this information provide context or background the audience requires?
- What is likely to happen if I don't include this information?
- Is this information included because it is second nature to me as the subject matter expert?

> ## Decipher This
>
> Many U.S. states and the federal government have enacted plain language laws that require public-facing material to be easily understandable and usable. The paragraph below was the first to come under fire after New York enacted its legislation in 1977.
>
> *Original*
>
> The liability of the bank is expressly limited to the exercise of ordinary diligence and care to prevent the opening of the within-mentioned safe deposit box during the within-mentioned term, or any extension or renewal thereof, by any person other than the lessee or his duly authorized representative and failure to exercise such diligence or care shall not be inferable from any alleged loss, absence, or disappearance of any of its contents, nor shall the bank be liable for permitting a co-lessee or an attorney in fact of the lessee to have access to and remove the contents of said safe deposit box after the lessee's death or disability and before the bank has written knowledge of such death or disability.
>
> Can you figure out what this means? How would you make it concise? The former 121-word sentence was more than cut in half:
>
> Our liability with respect to property deposited in the box is limited to ordinary care by our employees in the performance of their duties in preventing the opening of the box during the term of the lease by anyone other than you, persons authorized by you or persons authorized by the law.

> ### By the Numbers
>
> Sixty-five percent of people surveyed for *The State of Business Writing, 2016* said these are the top two problems with the writing they received:
>
> - It's too long
> - It's poorly organized

A Few Final Thoughts—Succinctly Put

It's important for us as communicators to take a close, critical, and considerate look at what we say and how we say it. When it comes to conciseness, however, brevity may be imposed on us. Conferences, meetings, roundtables, panel discussions, and other oral presentation formats have for decades (if not longer) restricted speakers to a specific length of time. Often there was no enforcement of this requirement and the 40-minute presentation we were expecting drifts, usually painfully, into 65 minutes. More and more, speakers are given a five-minute warning, then a two-minute warning as the moderator or organizer moves to the podium or the next item on the agenda.

Today many forms, grant applications, entrance requirements, and more limit word length (as well as font and font size). For example, you may be asked to explain how your project will ensure more people get affordable access to spinach, and not the lesser cousin kale. Instead of being allowed to wax eloquently about the origin of *Spinacia oleracea* in Persia, you're allotted 150 words at which point an online system will simply refuse to accept any more text.

Several years ago, a client of mine was complaining bitterly about his new boss (who was admittedly in the job he applied for and did not get). He wanted to demonstrate her silliness and rigidity. This was the example he used.

> Staff had received an e-mail that said all material over two pages had to come with a one-page summary. My client had a 10-page report, and he wrote a summary that was one paragraph over the one-page limit.

His boss thanked him for the report and asked for a one-page summary.

My client e-mailed back to clarify, somewhat snarkily I presume, that his boss wanted him to take the one-page, one-paragraph summary and reduce it to one page.

His boss wrote back, seemingly nicely, to say, "That's right."

My client felt this was a prime example of how his new boss made absurd requests.

But was it? What happens if the boss accepted a summary longer than one page, albeit by very little. How long would the next summary be? And the one after that?

I applauded his new boss. Secretly.

People are digging in their heels when it comes to wordiness. It wastes time and does not add value to the communication. They're busy, and they don't have time for communications that ramble and meander. They also don't want to have to work to understand a message or be drawn into content. And concise writing is more compelling.

Take a look.

This example is from an article by Laura Kelly on *The Readable Blog*, which according to a metric they use to measure readability is easily readable by only 25 percent of the general public.

There is currently a lively, ongoing controversy among many sociologists and other professionals who study human nature: theories are being spun and arguments are being conducted among them about what it means that so many young people—and older people, for that matter—who live in our society today are so very interested in stories about zombies. (58 words, 1 sentence)

How would you make it concise and much more interesting? Here's what *The Readable Blog* did:

A lively societal debate rages among the human sciences. The contentious issue is: why are so many people fascinated by zombie fiction?

And just like that, no more deadly prose.

> ### Try Your Hand—Revised
>
> Original
>
> 1. If the State Secretary finds that an individual has received a payment to which the individual was not entitled, whether or not the payment was due to the individual's fault or misrepresentation, the individual shall be liable to repay to State the total sum of the payment to which the individual was not entitled. (54 words)
>
> Revised
>
> If the State agency finds that you received a payment that you weren't entitled to, you must pay the entire sum back. (22 words)
> According to plainlanguage.gov, this example demonstrates conciseness techniques that more than halved the length of the original paragraph with no loss of meaning.
>
> Original
>
> 2. When the process of freeing a vehicle that has been stuck results in ruts or holes, the operator will fill the rut or hole created by such activity before removing the vehicle from the immediate area. (36 words)
>
> Revised
>
> If you make a hole while freeing a stuck vehicle, you must fill the hole before you drive away. (19 words)

As PLAIN notes, using simple, straightforward language helps us say what we mean without extra word clutter.

Original

3. This is a multipurpose passenger vehicle which will handle and maneuver differently from an ordinary passenger car, in driving conditions which may occur on streets and highways and off road. As with other vehicles of this type, if you make sharp turns or abrupt maneuvers, the vehicle may roll over or may go out of control and crash. You should read driving guidelines and instructions in the Owner's Manual, and WEAR YOUR SEAT BELTS AT ALL TIMES. (77 words)

Revised

A picture says in 19 words what originally took 77. And the message is clearer.

CHAPTER 4

Substance Abuse

Content that works for you—and for your audience

We have a lot to say. All too often, however, our message gets lost, and what we have to say goes unnoticed or misunderstood.

One issue: our communication fails to stand out from the crowd. And it is crowded out there. According to the Worldwide E-mail User Forecast, e-mail users received an average of roughly 4,000 e-mails in 2020. This figure is expected to approach 4,300 by 2022.

In his 2019 article "How to Spend Way Less Time on Email Every Day" in the *Harvard Business Review*, Matt Plummer notes that, on average, professionals have more than 200 e-mails in their inbox and receive 120 new ones each day. They respond to only 25 percent of them.

Two factors are linked to getting lost in the crush and the rush: a focus on the reader and a focus on the language we use. Let's start with the former.

If a Tree Falls …

The basic communications process looks like this:

> Sender: We need someone or something to be able to transmit our information.
> Message: We have to have something to say. (Ideally, something meaningful.)
> Medium: There must be some way to convey our message (phone, text, face to face, etc.).
> Receiver: There has to be someone or something on the other end to get our message.

All four components are critical to effective communication. Remember the paradoxical question "If a tree falls in the forest and there is no one there to hear it, does it make a sound?" Philosophers and audiologists may debate the answer; for communicators, there is no debate. If there is no one to receive our message, we have failed to communicate. We have wasted our time, and we have not achieved our purpose.

That helps to underscore why the receiver is the most important part of the communications process. Marketers have known this for some time. If you're trying to sell a tampon, having a male voiceover isn't going to win you clients. On the other hand, if you're selling a pregnancy test, images of happy parents of both sexes will earn kudos.

Imagine you sell cars, and you have this beautiful, red convertible at a great price. While we don't want to stereotype here, your first prosect is a 54-year-old recently divorced man. Your second prospect is a 21-year-old female university student. Your key message to both is the same: this is a great car—and it is a great car for you.

The information you give to the man, however, will not be the same as the info you give to the college student. Because they are not interested in the same things. What's relevant to one is not relevant to the other. If we want them to listen, if we want to convince them, we need to tailor our message to them. In this case, perhaps potential buyer #1 wants to know about pick-up on the highway while potential buyer #2 is interested in fuel efficiency.

As obvious as this sounds, many messages focus more on the sender, why we are reaching out, what we need, what we'd like our audience to do, how we feel, what we expect. Receivers will not find themselves reflected in these messages and will usually move on to messages that show an interest in them.

Distractions and Gnats

In many of the presentations I give and courses I teach, people will raise the issue of inconsiderate readers (usually) who don't respond by a given deadline despite the fact that the message has clearly stated a timely response is important. The thinking is the receiver of the message is at fault here, they have not taken our message seriously, they have neglected to do what was asked of them. From the reader's perspective, however, the message did two things that led to their lack of interest.

First, it showed why the request was important to the writer. It did not explain why this should also be important to the reader. Second, we as the writer assume our message goes to the top of the reader's pile. It rarely does unless we train readers, and listeners, that communications from us will be clear and relevant to them.

Our audience brings to every communication, whether written or spoken, two realities:

- They are distracted and usually multitasking.
- They have the attention span of a gnat.

Joshua Bell demonstrated this clearly in 2007. The world-renowned violinist, who made his Carnegie Hall debut at the age of 17, made his way to an arcade outside a Metro station in Washington, DC, with his $3.5 million Gibson Stradivarius in tow. For 43 minutes, he played six intricate and spell-binding pieces from some of the world's greatest composers. There were 1,097 people who walked by.

How many do you think stopped to listen?

Seven.

Two days before his visit to the DC subway station, Bell played a sold-out show in Boston. The average seat price: $100.

It's not that people don't like music or that they don't want to be spellbound by a virtuoso. But people—the people we are communicating with—are busy, they're rushing from one task to another, they're thinking about their to-do list, they're running for a bathroom having, unfortunately, eaten a kale salad for lunch. In the middle of this mayhem and multitasking, we enter with our message. We don't have a lot of time to get our audience's attention, and we have to work hard to keep it. Clarity and conciseness will help here. So will a focus on the audience.

One way to determine whether we have achieved this is to take a look at a presentation or piece of writing. How many times did we say, "I," "me," "this organization," "our?" How many times did we say "you?" The latter speaks directly to the audience and draws them in. The former says they really aren't important and that this message isn't really about them. (Of course, we will use this pronoun prudently. Telling someone, "You are an idiot," is likely to get a response, just not the one we wanted.)

Taking Center Stage

In writing, the audience focus is often referred to as reader-based prose. The opposite is writer-based prose, which centers on the writer's needs and emotions. We know how far that gets us.

More broadly, efforts to put the audience front and center use an approach called the "You Attitude." In many cases, our piece of writing or our presentation is clear and concise, it's just not inclusive language. This can often be changed easily and quickly. Like this:

> *I Attitude:* I wanted to send my sincere thanks for meeting such a tight deadline with the spinach harvest.
> *You Attitude:* Thank you for meeting such a tight deadline with the spinach harvest.
> *I Attitude:* We will start canning the spinach this week, and we will have the canning completed by June 10th.
> *You Attitude:* Your spinach is being canned this week, and you should receive the shipment by June 10th.
> *I Attitude:* We are pleased to offer a 10% discount on the spinach order. We do this for special customers.
> *You Attitude:* As a special customer, you will receive a 10 percent discount.

The You Attitude is just that: a perspective. We hear about patient-centered care and customer-centered service. For communications, this is about putting the people we're reaching out to at the heart of the communication. We need to do that respectfully, of course. (Hence, "You are an idiot," is not recommended.)

More Than Words

Consideration is about more than the language we use. It's a philosophy. Inherent in that philosophy is respect. Saying "please" and "thank you"—sincerely—is appreciated by audiences. It draws them in to a communication, builds trust, and increases engagement. All too often such common courtesies are overlooked, not because we're not nice people but because we are in a hurry, we're multitasking, we're distracted.

A course participant once told me one result of a survey that had hit home to her. The government she worked for conducted an employee feedback survey every two years. One question asked respondents to identify the things that discouraged them most about their job. The top answer: No one ever says thank you.

It's a little thing, and it makes such a big impact. That is the impact that comes from putting your receiver in the spotlight.

It's not hard to do. As a communicator, you need to know your audience, their needs, their knowledge level, their attitude about an issue. Even when we don't know our audience personally, we can usually put ourselves in their shoes. Most of us have shared an experience that mirrors our audience. We have been a customer, a patient, a student, a frustrated driver, even an opponent of kale.

Case Study

Several years ago, we did some work for a client, a government agency that was rewriting its form letters in response to new legislation. That legislation mandated a different calculation for benefits paid to workers injured on the job. The calculation wasn't easy, and it was a significant departure from the previous system.

The Client Services department spent a lot of time and effort working on a letter that would explain clearly and simply, without being condescending, how benefits were determined. This was important information, and they wanted to be sure injured workers understood how their monthly benefit was calculated. Also, the detailed explanation gave injured workers an opportunity to check the stated amount to ensure it was correct.

When we received the form letter, we put together a number of focus groups with workers who had been previously injured. We wanted them to review the material to make sure it was straightforward, understandable, and helpful. Without fail, every focus group said there was one major problem with the letter.

Can you guess what it was?

Nowhere in the letter did it say, "So sorry to hear you've been injured at work."

The Next-Friday Syndrome

Demonstrating why something is relevant to an audience, particularly spelling out how they will benefit—from responding to an e-mail, answering our questions, even eating spinach—is more likely to get us the results/response we were hoping for.

The You Attitude will enable us to speak directly to our audience, draw them into the content, and keep them there.

Another critical element: specificity.

Too often we rely on ambiguous, vague, and imprecise language. This will not win us friends and influence people. Rather it will bore, confuse, and mislead people.

One reason we default to words that don't state exactly what we mean and what we need is because we know the material we are communicating. We know why we're reaching out and what we want. It's a You Attitude issue. It's not about whether we understand this, but will our audience understand this.

Remember Dick Wadd from the first chapter who asked for a date next Friday? You see where that got him. That miscommunication is an example of using language that is open to interpretation because there is more than one reasonable conclusion to reach. If he'd said "this week," for example, there would only have been one possible interpretation.

This type of communication problem is called lexical ambiguity. It's when words have more than one meaning. As the sender, we always interpret the meaning as intended because it's our message. Audiences don't have that advantage.

In some cases, our audience will figure it out. Take this paragraph from J.D. Salinger's fabulous novel *The Catcher in the Rye*.

> I ran all the way to the main gate, and then I waited a second till I got my breath. I have no wind, if you want to know the truth. I'm quite a heavy smoker, for one thing—that is, I used to be. They made me cut it out. Another thing, I grew six and a half inches last year. That's also how I practically got t.b. and came out here for all these goddam checkups and stuff. I'm pretty healthy though.

Now let's read it again, focusing in on two words:

> I ran all the way to the main gate, and then I waited a second till I got my breath. I have no wind, if you want to know the truth. I'm quite a heavy smoker, for one thing—that is, I used to be. **They** made me cut it out. Another thing, I grew six and a half inches last year. That's also how I practically got t.b. and came out **here** for all these goddam checkups and stuff. I'm pretty healthy though.

What do these bolded words refer to? (Now admittedly, we are not in the middle of reading the novel, but give it your best shot.) It's usually assumed "they" refers to medical professionals and "here" to the mental health center where the main character Holden Caulfield is presumed to be staying.

Many readers of *The Catcher in the Rye* will reach this conclusion, correctly we assume. There is a technical term in communications for when audiences take an ambiguous word or phrase and arrive at the expected interpretation. We call it "guessing." Such nuance may be appropriate, even intriguing, in literary fiction. In workplace communications, it is simply annoying—and a major reason why our messages fail.

Guessing is dangerous. We run the real risk, that our audiences will attribute a meaning to our words that we never intended. This leads to miscommunication, and that, in turn, often requires additional communication to clarify. More wasted time, and not great for our reputation.

Guesswork may also require our audiences to slow down and divert from the main message while they interpret what it is we're saying. Readers and listeners don't have the time or the patience for that. They might do it once, after that they're moving on to clear, concrete communication—from someone else.

Double Entendre

There is another type of ambiguity that crops up regularly in communications. It's called syntactic or structural ambiguity and refers to there being two or more meanings for a sentence or phrase. Take this example:

Popeye spied Brutus with a telescope.

So what does this sentence mean? (1) That Popeye, our sailor man, was using a telescope to keep an eye on his arch nemesis. (2) That Popeye, ever diligent, got a bead on the big, bad Brutus, who, by the way, just happened to be carrying a telescope. (For no good deed, we're sure.)

The only person who can know the answer to the question is the writer/speaker. The arrangement of the words lend themselves—accurately—to either interpretation. Such problems can often be fixed easily.

Like this:

Using his telescope, Popeye spied Brutus.
Popeye spied Brutus, who was carrying a telescope.

We noted earlier that many readers and listeners will attempt to decipher the meaning of ambiguous language. Many won't. Like my friend, they'll assume they know what is meant by the phrase "next Friday," and blithely go about their day.

Dastardly Language

Ambiguous language can also lead to inaccurate interpretations. This, in turn, can lead to assumptions and conclusions never intended in the original sentence. Just ask Popeye and Olive Oyl.

Popeye did not go to the regatta because Olive Oyl was there.

This sentence has two possible meanings. It could mean that Popeye stayed away from the regatta because he knew that Olive Oyl would be there. That leads us to think Popeye and OO are on the outs. Which likely means they had a fight. Maybe because he is cheating on her. The bastard!

The second possible meaning is that Popeye didn't go to the regatta to see OO. He went for some other reason. Perhaps to confront Brutus about the telescope. I mean why does a landlocked sailor need a telescope—unless he's spying on someone. Someone like Olive Oyl. The bastard!

Less dramatic, but equally problematic, are the assumptions our readers and listeners—as well as ourselves—bring to sentences that are open to interpretation. For instance, if someone says, "I've never eaten spinach cooked this way," what might that mean to most people? What is it likely to mean to the chef?

It could be taken as a compliment. It could be taken as a criticism. Although the comment is straightforward enough, it opens the door to further interpretation.

As a journalist, I have written articles for hundreds of magazines and newspapers, both online and in print. It's not unusual for someone to say to me, "I read your article in *Spinach Monthly*" or "I saw your piece about thongs on *Beach Bums*." Invariably I say, "Thank you."

But what am I thanking them for? Neither comment actually says the person liked my article or thought it was well-written. Is that compliment implicit in the sentence? Maybe. Or maybe it's the speaker's way of acknowledging my work without having to say they liked it, because, well, they didn't. This is a different kind of ambiguity. One the Thong Principle rails against.

Poetic License

So how do we sidestep unclear language, avoid ambiguity, and bring precision to our words. Start with this fundamental tenet: My communication will have only one interpretation—the one I intended.

Here's the caveat to concrete writing and speaking. There are times we want nuance, or we want to be clever and compel our audience to think about the layers inherent in our language. Poetry does this as a matter of course. Take a look at the last line of this amazing poem.

Harlem
By Langston Hughes

What happens to a dream deferred?

Does it dry up
like a raisin in the sun?
Or fester like a sore—
And then run?

> Does it stink like rotten meat?
> Or crust and sugar over—
> like a syrupy sweet?
>
> Maybe it just sags
> like a heavy load.
>
> Or does it explode?

This powerful ending could mean that the dream explodes. It exists no more. It could mean that the dream explodes into power and passion and is more alive than ever before. It could mean a violent explosion, such as the Harlem riots of 1935 and 1943. It could, and probably does, mean all three. Hughes wanted the line to be open to interpretation. This wasn't accidental.

That is what we're trying to avoid, however, when we communicate for work—the unintended message. Hence, the mantra: one communication, one interpretation.

Through the Fog

A related issue to ambiguity is vagueness. In their book, *Critical Thinking: An Introduction to the Basic Skills* (5th ed. Broadview Press, 2008), William Hughes and Jonathan Lavery point to standard political pledges as an example of deliberately vague language. For example:

> My officials are monitoring this situation very closely, and I can promise that we shall take all appropriate measures to ensure that the situation is resolved in a way that is fair to all the parties involved.

That may make us feel better until we look at exactly what was said. How is the situation being monitored? What are appropriate measures? Who decides what is "fair"?

This vague language leads people to reach their own conclusions about what is meant, frequently arriving at the wrong conclusion. This, in turn, leads to feelings of having been misled, perhaps intentionally. Now we have another, often bigger, problem: lack of trust.

There are tactics that will help us avoid misinterpretation caused by words that don't clearly articulate their intent. Perhaps the simplest, the most straightforward—and the most overlooked—option is to replace vague language (and vague thinking) with specific details. Take, for example, this common sentence:

It's hot out.

On the surface, a basic, understandable sentence. But what does it actually mean? Unfortunately, different things to different people. If you live in Alaska, "hot" has a different connotation than if you live in Hawaii. "Hot" also varies depending on the time of year. A hot day in winter is unlike a hot day in August.

Such issues don't arise with this sentence:

It's 86 degrees out.

There is no misinterpretation. People in Alaska might think (at least before climate change), "Wow, that's sweltering!" Those in Hawaii might shrug, "Another typical day in July." But both understand exactly what the sentence means.

Facts and figures play a central role in ensuring precision of language. They make the message clearer and easier to understand on first reading/hearing. They bring credibility to the issue and the sender.

Compare these two examples.

- Popeye is worried that today's youth don't eat enough spinach.
- Only 22 percent of today's teenagers eat at least one leafy green vegetable a day——a reality that concerns Popeye.

Because concrete language is powerful, it is more persuasive. The accurate use of statistics, research findings, data, numbers, and more will convince audiences that what we're telling them is reliable, fact-based, and believable.

Elevated language is also at play here. The more erudite (ahem) the words, the more the meaning is open to interpretation and the less power it has. A speechwriter for Franklin Delano Roosevelt wrote this sentence:

We are trying to construct a more inclusive society.

FDR added this line:

We're going to make a country in which no one is left out.

Clearer and more impactful. Many people think the fancier, wordier, vaguer way of writing and speaking is more impressive. It isn't, and we'll explore why further in the chapter on plain language.

Taking Action

Another technique successful communicators use to make language crisp and concrete is to put action in their verbs. Verbs are the heart of a sentence. Indeed, they are the only words that can stand alone as a complete sentence. (Go! Halt! Run!) Given the importance and power of verbs, why would we mute them or bury them.

Just as the name implies, action verbs describe an action. For example:

Popeye grazes on spinach all day long; he crushes cans with one fist; and he swoons when Olive Oyl enters a room.

Action verbs are different from what are called linking verbs. These verb types can't depict action. Take for instance this sentence: Popeye was sad to learn kale consumption has increased worldwide.

The use of action verbs adds both oomph and precision to our communication. The same is true of words that paint a picture, convey a strong image or feeling, and stand out from the routine language of the workplace.

Everyday language
This is important.

Stronger language
This is critical.

The sentences are the same length and deliver a similar message, but one does so with a punch. That said, if all our communication becomes "critical," our audiences will soon see this as ordinary language and its impact will diminish. As well, the issue really must be critical, or our credibility is affected.

Now as professionals, we're not out to write a novel or win a Pulitzer, but that does not mean our language cannot be evocative and resonate with receivers. It's to our advantage when it does because they are more likely to listen or read what we have to say, understand it instantly, and—this is big—they're more likely to remember our message. And us.

Decipher This

Not So Great

Concerns about computerization cover a spectrum of diverse emotions. These include fears that the physical landscape in which people work will be degraded and that social connections will dissipate. There is a widespread belief that technology will be superior to human effort, and people will be devalued. However, as individuals become more knowledgeable about the attributes and abilities of automation, these concerns diminish.

Better

So why exactly are employees afraid of technology? They believe their workplaces will become cold and sterile; that they will not have social connections; and that their contribution will be diminished. They are afraid computers will make their work less necessary and important. This anxiety, however, tends to go away as technology becomes a more familiar part of the workplace.

Best

Technology is scary for many people—at least at first. Employees fear they'll be cut off from coworkers, that the workplace will become impersonal, that their work will suffer. However, as employees become more comfortable with computers, these fears disappear.

> ## By the Numbers
>
> According to widely published reports, a research study by Microsoft Corp., found that people have shorter attention spans than goldfish. That would be eight seconds for humans and nine seconds for goldfish.
>
> There is at least one article that contends this is fake news, and the statistic may not be accurate. What is most important though is the reaction to the goldfish analogy. There may be an initial surprise, but people quickly shrug and say, "Yep. That sounds about right."
>
> This is the world in which we communicate.

CHAPTER 5

It's Not What You Say, It's How You Say It, Idiot

The truth about tone

Words convey meaning. They also carry a tone. Often when we miscommunicate, it's not because of what we said but how we said it—or how we were perceived to have said something.

Readers and listeners react to messages in two ways: rationally and emotionally. The former is usually associated with content. Did the information we provide make sense? Did it make a lightbulb turn on? Did it convince someone? Did it help with decision making?

Tone is often connected to the emotional response audiences have to a message. This can be positive, negative, or neutral. Ideally, we'd like people to not only understand and appreciate what we have to say, but how we say it. A positive reaction benefits both the sender and the receiver. It builds trust, it helps create and maintain attention, it opens the door to fruitful discussions.

A negative reaction does the reverse. Indeed, as readers and listeners we get caught up in our emotional reaction to a message, often without being aware of what has set us off. But while we are fuming, disagreeing, feeling embarrassed, or any other negative response, we are not paying attention to the message, and we are not open to the content conveyed in that message. And as communicators, will have a less receptive reader or listener the next time we reach out.

Noise Maker

The emotional impact of what we say cannot be underemphasized. The amazing poet Maya Angelou once said, "I've learned that people will forget what you said, people will forget what you did, but people will never forget how you made them feel."

That's what tone does. It makes people feel unworthy or applauded. It makes people feel heard or dismissed. It makes people feel ignored or welcome. The choice is up to us.

Here's what happens when a negative tone intrudes on a message:

Dick Wadd asks my friend out for next Friday. When he calls to find out why she is not at the appointed place at the appointed hour, he snaps, "Where are you?"

My friend responds to the tone—not the content. We've all been asked nicely or curiously or eagerly, "Where are you?" That elicits a different response than the one Dick received. My friend picks up on his annoyance and reacts to the perceived or intended slap on the wrist. It's all downhill from there, and she marries someone else. One of the many implications of inappropriate tone.

But let's break this down further. Dick Wadd asks with obvious displeasure, "Where are you?"

While my friend is responding—and while the conversation is continuing—my friend is thinking to herself something like this: "What the frig is wrong with you? Next Friday doesn't mean this Friday, idiot. If you meant this Friday, why didn't you say that? Oh right, you're not that bright."

This internal dialogue, usually conducted at breakneck speed and full volume, is called noise. As communicators, we want to avoid noise. It takes our audience away from the message and coats the communication in a tenor that detracts from our content and our chance of success.

This is noise:

Try getting a message through this. It's unlikely any or much of what you have to say, in print or in person, will make it through. To get a message across successfully, we need to minimize noise.

Call center staff are often taught this. Don't answer an angry customer's questions. Don't provide information to an upset client. Don't give details to a distraught caller. Until you calm them down. Once that happens, the message is more likely to get through in the way we intended.

This is attention:

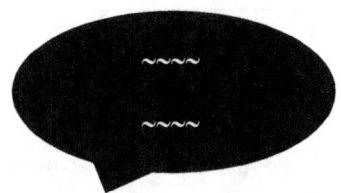

Tone is not about people being sensitive. It's about people being human. We need to understand that, and we need to respect it. We also need to be strategic in how we communicate knowing what we do about the impact of tone on an individual. The You Attitude helps here.

The Human Connection

The significant effect tone has on an audience is not surprising. A 2016 study conducted by Ruvanee Vilhauer at New York University found that more than 80 percent of people hear an inner voice while they read. They are finding the human in our communication. If what we have to say sounds cold, indifferent, dismissive, or otherwise negative, readers will react to that because they can hear us in their heads. Listeners have the same reaction although we have a greater opportunity to enhance tone when we are speaking.

Here are three numbers for you: 7, 38, 55

Here are three elements of communication: words, gestures, voice

Now match up the number with the corresponding communication element. This is how people interpret what we're saying—regardless of what we may have intended. What element carries the most weight? The least?

In his classic book *Silent Messages* (1971), author Albert Mehrabian, a psychology professor at the University of California, Los Angeles, determined that the communications component people relied on the most to derive meaning from a message was gestures and body language. The least important was the words themselves. So our chart looks like this:

Element of communication	Importance in interpreting a message
Gestures and facial expressions	55%
Tone of voice	38%
Words	7%

We need to remember this when we speak and when we write. If we stand stiffly before our colleagues in a meeting and look down at our notes, not making eye contact, what message are we sending about our confidence in our content and ourselves—regardless of what it is we might actually be saying. Likewise, a well-crafted letter that sounds distant or condescending conveys a tone that supersedes the words themselves.

It is essential to determine in advance not only what we want to say but how we want those words to sound. If we misstep, audiences will turn inward, noise will dominate, and our message will fail to achieve its purpose. We'll be forced to communicate again or find another solution for our issue.

The impact of tone cannot be underestimated. Try this exercise. It will require you to put aside your cell phone, your iPad, your laptop, and even your grandmother's hardcover dictionary. On the next page, you'll find six words. Try to find another, simpler word or phrase to use in their place. For example, if the word is "uncomplicated," you might replace that with "simple" or "not hard." Before you tackle the translation, write down (yes, write it) the number of words you think you'll be able to change easily.

Here we go.

Replace these words with clearer, easier words or phrases:

Rectitude

Propitious

Laconic

Lamina

Callow

Glabrous

So how did you do? Did you translate, easily, as many words as you thought? Most of us don't.

Most of us go into an exercise like this thinking we'll do well, if not exceptionally well. After all, we're bright, we're professionals, we work in demanding jobs, we have a command of the English language. And yet, we don't know what "glabrous" means. And why should we. When was the last time that came up in conversation Friday night over a beer. That would be never.

This exercise serves as a reminder of the danger of lofty language. When our readers and listeners don't understand the words we use—because they are elevated, technical, or jargon—they are forced to ignore what we are saying or guess at our meaning. Neither option moves us any closer to getting our message across accurately. (Yes, they could look it up and get distracted in the process. And aside from this exercise, when was the last time you rushed to look up a word?)

The Inner Circle

This exercise also serves to highlight the issue of tone. Every time someone writes or speaks to us, we paint them with a brush of humanity. Audiences make it clear they don't want to talk to the company, the government, the hospital, the court. They want to communicate with a human being, and if we don't consciously communicate this human side, our audience will give us the attributes they glean from our content, our organization of information, and our use of language.

Try this out. Let's attribute tone to the six words you deciphered. What kind of person would write or speak like that? Would they wear jeans and a t-shirt? A tweed jacket? A bow tie? What would they do for a living? Belly or ballroom dancer? Would they give a "talk" or a "lecture?"

This is not about stereotyping; it's about understanding what our audience does inadvertently and automatically when we communicate with them.

It is very difficult to convey to audiences, for example, that we are down to earth, helpful, and open to ideas when we use language such as "propitious" and "callow." It says to our audiences that there is a special group of people that speak and write like this, and they are not part of that special group. So from the outset we have created a message that excludes the people we are talking to. In essence, we're saying, "You don't belong here." This is, of course, the antithesis of the You Attitude.

Language that is formal, difficult, highbrow, and full of specialized terms and jargon is often called "bureaucratic language." Audiences respond to this language the same way we responded to the 40-page report on our office chair. And we train the people we communicate with to listen to our messages or ignore them. If we make our communication difficult and distant, they will stop opening our e-mails and paying attention to our presentations.

So, remember those six words. Let's see how you did—and how we could do better by simplifying the language.

Rectitude—Decency, Honesty
Propitious—Hopeful, Promising
Laconic—Brief, Curt
Lamina—Casing, Coating
Callow—Naïve, Immature
Glabrous—Bare, Shaven

Language clearly affects tone. So does length. Shorter sentences by their very nature are more emphatic. This can be interpreted as abruptness, even rudeness. For example, if you are upset with a colleague, you could say:

I'd like to review the discussion in the meeting today. There were some comments about spinach I found concerning.

Or you could say:

Bite me.

Not a verbatim translation, admittedly, but you see the difference in tone. Longer is softer. So if you want to be friendly, conciliatory, open, opt for a longer sentence. This doesn't violate the principle of conciseness because the extra words are necessary to achieve the right tone. It's all about putting the focus on the person or people you are communicating with.

How Rude

Many senders are surprised by what annoys, offends, and irritates their receivers. We shouldn't be. This disconnect between how we think we sound and how our words are interpreted happens because we don't take a step back. We get caught up in what we want to say, on how much time we have before the next meeting, on the importance of the message to us. Nowhere in there is our reader or our listener. We have not looked at the message from the audience's point of view.

Many of us will think tone is not an issue. We're nice people; we're respectful; we're good. Chances are we're still emitting a tone that rankles.

In *Cycle to Civility*, a working paper published by Christine Porath, an associate professor of management at the McDonough School of Business at Georgetown University in Washington, DC, the author notes that the percentage of employees who report being treated rudely has grown by 13 percentage points since 1998, from 49 to 62 percent. According to Porath, poor communications is a key factor, and in a digital age, messages are prone to communication gaps and misunderstanding.

Clearly we need to be aware of what we have to say and how we say it.

By the Numbers

An article in the *Harvard Business Review* by Christine Porath and Christine Pearson in 2013 cited the results of a poll of 800 managers and employees in 17 industries who had been on the receiving end of incivility. Here's how they reacted:

- 48 percent intentionally decreased their work effort.
- 47 percent intentionally decreased the time spent at work.
- 38 percent intentionally decreased the quality of their work.
- 80 percent lost work time worrying about the incident.
- 63 percent lost work time avoiding the offender.
- 66 percent said that their performance declined.
- 78 percent said that their commitment to the organization declined.
- 12 percent said that they left their job because of the uncivil treatment.
- 25 percent admitted to taking their frustration out on customers.

Case Study

On April 9, 2017, Dr. David Dao Duy Anh, was forcibly removed from a United Airlines flight at Chicago O'Hare International Airport. While security officers were removing the passenger, his face was struck against an armrest, apparently knocking him out.

This is what Oscar Munoz, United Airlines CEO, said in a letter to employees about the controversial incident:

The situation was unfortunately compounded when one of the passengers we politely asked to deplane refused and it became necessary to contact Chicago Aviation Security Officers to help. Our employees followed established procedures for dealing with situations like this.

While I deeply regret this situation arose, I also emphatically stand behind all of you, and I want to commend you for continuing to go above and beyond to ensure we fly right.

This is what Munoz said in a public statement:

This is an upsetting event to all of us here at United. I apologize for having to re-accommodate these customers. Our team is moving with a sense of urgency to work with the authorities and conduct our own detailed review of what happened. We are also reaching out to this passenger to talk directly to him and further address and resolve this situation.

A few things to note:

- The difference in tone. The statement is warmer. It uses conversational language (with one notable exception).
- The letter uses vague language: "it became necessary" (Why?) "established procedures" (Which are?) "situations like this? (Dragging an unconscious man from a plane?). The statement is more exact: the company is doing its own review; the passenger will be contacted directly.
- The emphasis on "I" in the last sentence of the letter. What does this communicate to readers?

The tone difference is apparent. It's about conversational and concrete language. That said, there was one word in the statement that caused an uproar on social media. Can you find it? *Hint*: It's the word you have never used on Friday night over a beer.

That word, re-accommodate, raises an issue of trust as well as clarity. What does this word really mean in this context? Why can't the company just say what it actually means in a language we can easily understand? Are they trying to hide something?

The word caused such an uproar, *Time* magazine mused in an article it might win the award for Euphemism of the Year. That article pointed out Merriam-Webster reported searches for the word "re-accommodate" soared by 80,000 percent following the United Airlines CEO's statement.

> *Three days after the incident, this is what Munoz had to say during an interview on* Good Morning America*:*
> This will never happen again. We are not going to put a law enforcement official onto a plane … to remove a booked, paid, seated passenger. We can't do that.
> Message received.

Watch Your Tone

Do this:

- *Read your work out loud.* This will, literally, let you know how it sounds. This is particularly helpful when the issue is sensitive or controversial, you don't know your audience well, or the issue is important.
- *Take a break between writing and sending/speaking.* Distance will let you see what you're saying with new eyes. If the message is short, even a quick stretch or coffee refill will offer the opportunity of new awareness and perspective.
- *Focus on the audience.* Read what you have to say as if you were the intended receiver.
- *Ask a trusted colleague or friend for input.* If the document or presentation is potentially divisive, a second set of eyes and ears is helpful.
- *Edit for clarity and consideration.* Take another look at what you have to say. Is there anything that can be misinterpreted from a content or tone point of view? Revising is always important.

Don't do this:

Dash off a quick e-mail. This always makes us feel efficient. Until we have to communicate again. And perhaps apologize.

Wing the presentation. No matter your comfort level with speaking publicly or privately, knowing what you want to say—and how it should be said—is critical. We stumble when we are not prepared.

CHAPTER 6

Trust Me

This Is Fundamental

We've spent five chapters talking about the importance of communication and how to ensure our communication is effective and engaging. This chapter looks at why it may all be a waste of time.

There is an essential ingredient that enables us to achieve our communication purpose: trust. This is what makes our audiences more open to what we have to say and more willing to believe our message. In marketing, trust is often called "credibility." In public relations, it's "reputation." In communications, trust is called "goodwill." And without goodwill, it is unlikely we will communicate successfully. We certainly won't be able to communicate easily.

Our audience needs to be able to trust that we know what we are talking about. That's primarily a content, or rational, issue. They also need to be able to trust that we are being open and upfront with them. That is often a tone, or emotional, issue.

Remember Bill Clinton, who served as the 42nd president of the United States from 1993 to 2001. In 1998, he was impeached by the House of Representatives after denying, then un-denying, an affair with a 22-year-old White House intern, Monica Lewinsky. On the evening of Monday, August 17, 1998, Bill Clinton made a televised appearance before the American public, indeed the world. In that professionally delivered speech, he said, "I did have a relationship with Ms. Lewinsky that was not appropriate. In fact, it was wrong. It constituted a critical lapse in judgment and a personal failure on my part for which I am solely and completely responsible."

Response to the 548-word speech was divided. According to a CNN/USA Today/Gallup Poll, 51 percent of people believed Clinton gave an adequate apology; 44 percent felt he did not take responsibility for his actions. Yet the majority said they thought Clinton had committed perjury.

Why the divide? After all, everyone heard the same speech—the exact same words—delivered at the same time and place by the same person. The distinguishing factor is trust. If you turned on your TV as a Clinton supporter on this issue, you heard an honest, contrite human trying to make amends. If you didn't trust Clinton before the speech, you saw someone trying to sidestep his obligations. You heard someone who actually never apologized to the intern whose life he uprooted.

What the Research Tells Us

In an article in *Forbes* magazine in 2020, behavioral statistician Joseph Folkman shared the results of research he conducted to explore the issue of trust and communication. He and his colleagues had data about 97,872 leaders who had been evaluated on their effectiveness by 509,097 direct employee reports. Each employee was asked to rate the leader's ability to communicate effectively and on the issue of trust. They were also asked if they would "recommend this organization as a good place to work." The researchers found that leaders who rated low on communication but high in trust had direct reports who were significantly more likely to recommend their organization as a good place to work. Bottom line: Trust trumps even beautifully crafted communications.

Another article, "Communication, Commitment & Trust: Exploring the Triad," published in the *International Journal of Business and Management* in 2011 explored the relationship between communication, trust, and commitment. More than 240 employees from a mid-size food processing company in Australia were surveyed. The researchers found that the perceived effectiveness of communication between management and employees, commitment, pride in working for the company, and trust were significantly interrelated. However, the relationship between trust and communication was the strongest. The researchers concluded that, "[T]he study shows that trust and commitment do not just happen; they are forged and maintained through effective communication."

In her blog *Trust in the Workplace: Why It Is so Important Today and How to Build It*, Kristina Martic highlights the benefits of goodwill.

Ninety-six percent of engaged employees trust management compared with only 46 percent of disengaged employees. So what? Well, employees in highly trusted workplaces have 50 percent higher productivity, 106 percent more energy at work, and 13 percent fewer sick days. When there is trust, employees are 23 percent more likely to offer ideas and solutions.

Building Goodwill

Goodwill is earned. It doesn't happen automatically, and it can be easily damaged. Rebuilding can be time consuming and difficult. Savvy communicators will work to build and maintain goodwill—and that requires doing all the things we have discussed up to this point. Things such as putting a focus on the audience, keeping our messages concise and concrete, and using conversational language. Tone, of course, is critical here. It's hard to build trust when you've just ticked someone off.

It is important to put goodwill in context. When many people hear this word, they think they are being asked to be someone they're not. That defies the Thong Principle. Goodwill does ask us to be respectful, honest, and open. Nothing more. We don't have to like someone, we don't have to have coffee with someone, we don't have to shy away from difficult subjects. We can discipline employees, speak to colleagues about their inappropriate behavior, and fire someone if it comes to that. And we can do it all while maintaining goodwill.

What we can't do is pretend to be nice, pretend to care, pretend something isn't important, or that we are happy with the way things are progressing. Audiences will see right through that, and our credibility will be negatively affected. Indeed, the last thing audiences want is for us to beat around the bush or patronize them. It's like wearing a thong when every fiber of your body is calling out for trunks or a one-piece bathing suit.

A study conducted by researchers at Brigham Young University in 2017 found that when it comes to delivering bad news, candor is preferred to buttering up. Several bad news scenarios were given to 145 participants. They ranked how clear, considerate, direct, efficient, honest, specific, and reasonable they perceived the message to be. As well, they ranked which characteristics they valued most. Topping the list: clarity and directness.

Truth is most of us aren't rude. We don't mean to offend or devalue. We want to demonstrate that we are considerate, and we want to motivate those we work with. But we're busy, we get caught up in the moment, in the noise in our head, the demands of the day. We fail to build goodwill because we forgot, we were rushed, or we didn't think it was important.

Our audiences think otherwise. I routinely get e-mails from colleagues talking about projects we are jointly working on. Someone has a suggestion for next steps, or concerns about a particular component of the project. I tend to dive in. I'm driven to "solve" the problem. To keep us moving forward.

That stretch before hitting send that we discussed earlier often saves me. I realize I was focused on what I needed to achieve, on what I think should be done, on what works best for my schedule. That second look often reminds me to add a thank you for the person's suggestion or for raising their concerns. It sets a tone—one I believe we should set—and it builds goodwill. Sincerely.

It sounds so simple. It is. And it isn't. Goodwill is about wearing the swimwear that suits our personality, adding a splash of thoughtfulness, and making someone else the center of our attention. But we need to do this genuinely.

Little things make a big difference. An employee recognition survey conducted in 2016 by the Society for Human Resource Management and Globoforce found that organizations that spend just one percent of their payroll on thanking and recognizing their employees "are more likely to perceive greater impacts on retention and financial outcomes."

Another study, published in *The Magic Word for Business Growth Report*, involved more than 1,200 workers in the United Kingdom. Forty percent of respondents said they would feel less motivated to work hard if their employer did not say "thank you" or recognize their work. Nearly 50 percent said "rarely receiving any form of thanks or gratitude from their employer would make them want to leave the company."

But goodwill is about more than saying please and thank you, however heartfelt. If we are truly putting our audience on centerstage—because we are both considerate and strategic in attaining our goals—we need to move beyond nice language to action. Have we made the communication easy to read/hear, easy to follow? Have we made it clear and concise? Have we outlined benefits? Have we used an appropriate tone? Have we organized ideas and information logically and smoothly? Have we been forthright?

Four-Step Process for Organizing Information

Often when we sit down at the keyboard, fingers fly, then we hit the send button. A similar process often unfolds when we present. We think about what we want to say, stand up, open our mouth, and we're off.

This might work. We could end up with very effective communication that achieves our purpose and builds goodwill. It's more likely, however, that we'll end up forgetting something important, use words we wouldn't on second thought, use more words than necessary, and convey a tone we hadn't intended. The best approach to writing and speaking is to think before we communicate. This is especially important if we don't know our audience well, if the subject is lengthy or complex, or if the issue is sensitive.

Here is a four-step process that will help you identify what information should be included, how to organize that information, and the tone you want to convey to build goodwill. The components are:

Purpose
Audience
Key messages
Proof

Let's break them down.

Purpose

It's easy to get distracted. It's easy to veer away from our topic. If we understand clearly why we are communicating, we are more likely to stay on point. This helps with relevance and brevity. And it helps to build goodwill, since we are not wasting our audience's time or confusing the bejesus out of them.

It sounds like such a simple thing: Why am I writing? Why am I presenting? Too often, though, we are unclear about our purpose, perhaps because we have been tasked with communicating or are uncertain about what it is we need. If we are unclear, there is no way our communication can be clear. We'll talk about this more in a minute.

There are three reasons we communicate:

- To inform
- To persuade
- To entertain

We're not really interested here in the last reason. We're very interested in the first two. Learning is about the exchange of information. We're passing it along, or we are requesting it.

Persuading is about asking someone to act. We want to convince our audience to do something or to think something. Persuasion is a much more difficult type of communication than informing.

To ensure we create the content needed to achieve our purpose, we need to be able to state that purpose in one simple sentence. Goodwill is always inherent in our communication, so we do not need to state this as a goal.

For example, we might say:

The purpose of this presentation is to distinguish spinach from kale.

This report will document growth and future prospects in the thong industry.

I am writing this email to introduce J. Wellington Wimpy to the team.

Once our purpose is clear, we have a strong foundation on which to build the communication itself.

Audience

Too often we know who we're communicating with, but we haven't really thought about their needs. Focusing on our readers or listeners specifically helps us craft more effective messages.

There are two key aspects of our audience that we are interested in. First, what do we know about them? What is our relationship? Are they a colleague? A customer? A boss? Are we on a first-name basis? Friendly?

This will affect tone. Usually the better we know someone, the friendlier we can sound. We can be more informal, more conversational and casual. If we're not, it may be interpreted as us being dismissive or annoyed. The reverse is also true, if we don't know our audience well or the relationship is one of hierarchy, sounding too friendly will be off putting, or worse. See what happens when you e-mail your CEO or Deputy Minister with the opening line: Yo!

The second thing we want to know about our audience is their level of knowledge about the subject. The more they know, the less information we have to provide. The less they know, the more description, explanation, and examples will be needed. The more they know, the more we can use technical terms, jargon, and acronyms. The less they know, the plainer and more straightforward our language needs to be.

So now we know why we're communicating and with whom. It's time to figure out what to say.

Key Messages

As an expert, a specialist, a project manager, a supervisor, a great employee, we usually know a lot of details about the subject we're communicating. Our audience rarely needs—and certainly doesn't want—all those details. We have to narrow down what's necessary for them to know and what can safely be omitted. Key messages help us do just that.

Key messages are broad, general statements that summarize the main points of our communication. They're linked to our purpose. And they are few in number. We can't have 24 key messages. We'll leave our readers and our listeners in a fog.

So zero in on this: If our audience remembers only one or two things after hearing us speak or reading our message, what are the most important things we need them to remember? Those one or two things are our key messages.

Because key messages are general statements, we don't usually include them in our documents and presentations. We let the audience reach the conclusions we want them to reach or we might provide the key statement and then support it with this …

Proof

This is about concrete language. This is about offering data, statistics, facts, examples, testimonials, and more that demonstrate our point. We don't say something is important, we show that it is. We don't suggest something is a good idea, we prove it is.

In doing so, we build our credibility. And goodwill.

Now let's try the four-part process with an example. We need to write to a client who has lost a copy of their general liability insurance policy document. The client operates a 40-acre spinach farm and wants to review the policy to ensure they are covered for severe weather conditions. The client is still fully insured.

Here's the draft from one of our employees:

Subject line: Insurance policy #68957
Dear Policy Holder:
We have received your request for a copy of lost insurance policy #68957 dated August 12, 2021. We are unable to reissue a copy of the lost policy document until we verify the request. Please complete and return the attached form and return it to us by August 26, 2021. Once we have received the completed form, we will review it and respond.

Should you require additional information about your lost policy, please do not hesitate to contact Richard Wadd Insurance at 1-888-555-DENY. We look forward to hearing from you in the near future.

Sincerely,
Harold Hamgravy
Account Manager

So let's apply the four-step process and see what we might do differently.

Purpose

We could say the purpose is to respond. We could say the purpose is to send the form. They both sound pretty obvious (and bland), so let's dig a little deeper.

We're an insurance company. We're in a regulated industry. Chances are there are requirements governing communication with clients. It's likely if we don't get the form back in two weeks, we'll have to follow up. That's a waste of our time and money. There may even be a requirement to follow up a third and final time. More time and more money down the drain—and we didn't lose the damn document.

Even if we are not required to follow up, chances are we will. Business is competitive. We want to keep customers happy, because happy customers are loyal and they spend more.

According to Bain & Company, a management consulting firm based in Boston, a customer is four times more likely to go elsewhere if the problem is service-related than price- or product-related. The likelihood of selling to an existing customer is 60 to 70 percent, according to Marketing Metrics. The chances of selling to a new prospect: 5 to 20 percent.

So chances are we'll follow up. But we'd rather not do that, and we won't have to if the form gets filled out the first time. And there it is.

Our purpose: To get the form completed and returned.

Audience

Even if we don't know our audience personally, we know two things about them that are central to our message. First, they are a customer. This defines our relationship. They have expectations of us; we have obligations, legal and otherwise.

Of all the insurance companies, the spinach farmer picked us. We'll want to be helpful and effective, to the extent we can. (We still have to adhere to policy and procedures.) We'll want to reaffirm the customer picked the right company to do business with. Of course, we won't say any of that. It will be inherent in our tone and our content.

The second thing we know about our audience is that they have lost something, something potentially important and something connected to a large organization with policies, regulations, and other strictures. How does that make you feel? Think about losing your driver's license. What goes through your mind?

Does it sound like this:
Ohh, this is delightful. A chance to talk with the department of motor vehicles.
This is an opportunity to meet some new and wonderful people.

Or does it sound like this:
Dammit, this is exactly what I needed today. Another pain in the butt. I can't believe this happened. This is my husband's fault.

Invariably our thoughts are negative when we lose an important document. There is noise. The question we need to ask as communicators is what is causing the noise? We may not know our customer, but we have been in their shoes. Why would losing something like a driver's license or insurance policy cause negative thoughts? What is going through their mind?

Chances are they're worried replacing the policy is going to be a pain. But why? Here's what's eating at them:

How long will this take to replace?
How difficult will the process be?

How much will this cost?
Am I still insured?

Key Messages

Let's boil our messages down to their core. If readers remember nothing else, what two things do we need them to remember about our communication.

Think about our purpose. What do we need to achieve as the writer? Aha, there is a key message:

This form is important.

Now we're not going to tell readers that; we'll prove it to them. But this is the conclusion we want them to reach—the take-away.

The second key message is linked to our customer. What's going on with them? They're frustrated and on edge about replacing the policy. So what we do want to do: reassure. And there it is, key message #2.

This is not a big deal. Easy peasy, lemon cheesy.

Now, we are obviously not going to use these sentences, but we want to convey that message. What happens to people when we reassure them? They relax. In some cases, literally; you can hear them let out a long sigh and see their body loosen.

When that happens, we have their attention. Easy peasy.

Proof

So now we know what we need to say. We even have a starting point—reassurance. Next up: the facts, figures, and language that will support our key messages. So, let's jump in:

How do we demonstrate the form is important?

We make it easy to complete the form. Is there any information we can fill in in advance? Can we use an arrow or other tool to show them where to sign? Can we do it all online without having to make them print off a page, sign, and scan? The fact that we went to this effort shows the significance of the form.

We tie completing the form to what they want—a copy of their policy. As soon as we get the form back, they're one step closer to getting a copy of their policy.

How do we reassure the reader?
We answer their questions:

How long will this take to replace?
How difficult will the process be?
How much will this cost?
Am I still insured?

The more positive the responses to these questions, the easier the e-mail is to write and the more quickly we build goodwill. But if more steps are required before our customer gets their policy document, explaining why these steps are in place and what they are actually helps the reader and will also build goodwill.

So, now we know how to start our e-mail and what info to include. Something like this:

Dear Ms. Oyl:

Your general liability insurance policy can be easily replaced. All you need to do is complete the attached form. A replacement copy will be issued once the information is verified with our records on file; this usually takes 2–3 days. There is no charge for this service or the replacement copy, and your coverage remains intact.

If you have any questions, please contact me at my direct number below.

Sincerely,
Harold Hamgravy
Goodwill Ambassador

Let's Get Picky

We've covered a number of important communication issues and problems to this point. Let's delve into a few of those that are raised by this particular e-mail.

Conciseness reconsidered. Communications research—and our audiences—make it quite clear we waste words. We use 10 words where five will do. We create a 40-page document when a two-page infographic will work better. This example raises an issue of conciseness. The first version asks the customer to complete and return the form. Fair enough. That's linked directly to our purpose.

The conciseness principle, though, nudges us to ask if both words are required. How many people will complete the form and never return it because we didn't state this was required? The answer is likely very few. In that same vein, how many readers would take the uncompleted form and return it to us still blank? Same answer as the first question. So, the research and textbooks would encourage us to use one word ("complete" or "return") instead of three ("complete and return").

This is smart thinking. But the Thong Principle asks us to go a step further and ask, "In my world, what works best for me and my receiver?" Many course participants and students tell me their experience has shown them not only do they have to tell customers, clients, and members of the public to complete and return a form, they also have to tell them to sign it. Four words instead of one—but these four words serve as a reminder to the audience and get the sender closer to achieving their goal. These aren't wasted words; they are essential.

This is also an example of building goodwill. We have made it easier for our audience to comply, to understand, to agree. This, in turn, makes it easier for us to achieve our purpose.

Switching sides. The first e-mail refers, accurately, to the lost policy document. This is how we view the issue from the perspective of an insurance company and an account manager. This is the issue we have to address.

Now let's put on our thong. What happens to our reader every time we use the word "lost." Yup. It raises, even subtly, reminders of that situation. Remember, the dog barfed up a furball, the soup had a hair in it, and the damn policy was nowhere to be found. Referring to a "lost policy" is negative language. We want to avoid this if we can. So using only the word "policy" is a neutral option.

Here the Thong Principle nudges again. Neutral is better than negative. But could we actually make the language positive? Positive language is usually more concise and considerate, and we can do this. The key is to focus on what the reader wants, not what we want. The reader, our customer, wants a replacement copy. And there it is, the golden word. What happens every time we use the word "replacement"? Our reader smiles, they exhale, they relax. There might even be a dance of joy.

There is most certainly goodwill.

Editor's Pen

Since we're here, let's dissect Harold Hamgravy's draft e-mail.

Dear Policy Holder: *Accurate, and better than "Dear Sir or Madam," but still impersonal and not respectful of diversity. If we have the customer's account number, we have their name. Using someone's name makes the communication more powerful and direct.*

We have received [*focus on the sender not the receiver*] your request for a copy of lost [*Yeah, let's not open that door*] insurance policy #68957 [*The reader is unlikely to know or remember their policy number. They are more likely to remember the type of insurance: auto, home, general liability. If we need to record the policy number, put it in brackets, so it is downplayed.*] dated August 12, 2021. [*Again, the reader is unlikely to remember or care whether they contacted us on August 20th or the 21st. What they want is a quick and helpful response. If we need to include this info, put it in a footer at the bottom or beneath the e-mail signature. If we include the date, we need to be very careful we are not replying after a delayed period of time. There is nothing worse that reminding our audience we took four weeks to get back to them.*] We are unable to reissue a copy of the lost policy document [*What happens as soon as the reader hits this line? Noise. Better to start with the need to verify the signature.*] until we verify the request [*What does this mean? How do you verify the request? Do I need to do more work?*]. Please complete and return the attached form and return it to us by August 26, 2021. [*Why the deadline? This might be helpful information if there is a reason for the request. Otherwise it's just arbitrary.*] Once we have received the completed form, we will review it and respond. [*This means something to the writer. To the reader, it raises more questions. What are you reviewing? Why do you need to review it? What do you mean you'll respond? Why can't I get my insurance policy? If there really is a review process, we'll need to explain what is being reviewed, why, and how long it will take.*]

Should you require additional information about your lost policy, please do not hesitate [*a cliché or overused phrase that does not sound sincere given the distant and cool tone of the letter*] to contact Richard Wadd Insurance [*formal, not conversational or warm*] at 1-888-555-DENY. We look forward to hearing from you in the near future [*unnecessary and not believable*].

Sincerely,
Harold Hamgravy
Account Manager

By the Numbers

A 2017 study published in the *Harvard Business Review* found that people at high-trust companies—where goodwill abounds—fared much better than their counterparts at low-trust companies. They reported:

- 74 percent less stress
- 50 percent higher productivity
- 106 percent more energy at work
- 13 percent fewer sick days
- 76 percent more engagement
- 29 percent more satisfaction in their lives
- 40 percent less burnout

CHAPTER 7

Plain Language—Who Gives a Crap

Everyone apparently

The push to use plain language is substantial, and it's growing. In fact, plain language has become a global movement. Plain Language Association International (PLAIN), for example, includes members from over 30 countries working in at least 15 languages. In some of those countries, including the United States, plain language is now the law in many cases.

Plain language advocates are demanding change. That demand is linked to two issues we have already discussed. First, audiences can't figure out what the hell we're trying to say when we use elevated, bureaucratic, technical, dense, and difficult language. They're compelled to guess what we mean, ignore what we're saying, or turn to a dictionary, a thesaurus, and other lost souls. We fail to get our message across, and we cut away at whatever goodwill we had.

Goodwill is also linked to the second reason the plain language movement has gained a global audience: we don't trust organizations, particularly government and big business. That lack of trust means we want things stated clearly and concisely so everyone arrives at the same intended interpretation.

Plainly put, when we say what we mean and mean what we say, we convey our message simply and straightforwardly, we achieve our purpose, and we build goodwill. It's better than spinach.

Our starting point is understanding what is meant by plain language and how it differs from other forms of communication. At its heart, plain language is communication your audience can understand the first time they hear or read it. It doesn't need to be reread or rewound to comprehend it.

But plain language goes further. PLAIN says that for communication to be in plain language audiences must be able to:

- Find what they need
- Understand what they find
- Use what they find to meet their needs

This definition goes beyond what has traditionally been considered plain English, although there is significant overlap. Speaking and writing clearly, concisely, and considerately has been the mantra of many writers and orators for many centuries because it works. Here the focus is on the language and techniques such as using familiar words and keeping sentences shorter rather than longer.

Plain language focuses on the reader or the listener. The aim is to be clear, concise, and effective.

It is equally important to understand what plain language is not. These myths or misconceptions help to explain some of the resistance to plain language—and there is significant resistance. According to PLAIN, plain language is *not*:

1. Baby talk, or an attempt to be folksy, playful, or PC
2. Stripping out necessary technical and legal information
3. Just editorial "polishing" after you finish writing
4. Imprecise
5. Just using pronouns in a Q and A format
6. Something the lawyers will never go for
7. Easy

To that list, we must add that plain language is not condescending. This is not about speaking down to people because they are stupid. Indeed, it is the reverse. Because people are bright, they will see through attempts to use language to befuddle or mislead. Because people are busy and engaged, they will not waste their time on communication that confounds.

Quite simply, if we want our message to stand out from the crowd, we want to use plain language.

Benefits Package

When we use plain language, it's understood—and it's appreciated. The spotlight is on the audience, so we are more likely to engage listeners and readers, which means we are more likely to get our message across as intended. Barriers come down, understanding goes up. In the case of documents such as policies and regulations, this means compliance also goes up.

We recently completed a training program for a government department that oversees occupational health and safety. We were working with the safety inspectors. A tough job. Businesses and workers often don't like to see inspectors arrive, assuming it means bad news and more work. Required changes to the job site, as written up and explained in person, are often seemingly ignored.

During our discussion of plain language, one participant shared this story. He had inspected a construction site and the required inspection on one vehicle had lapsed. The inspector's report said the vehicle could not be used until it passed a maintenance check. When the inspector returned to the site, the vehicle was still in use and the inspection sticker on the windshield was the original lapsed one. The inspector spoke to the site supervisor to let him know the company was not compliant. The site supervisor disagreed. "We've made all your changes."

The inspector pointed to item #5, "Industrial sideloader does not have up-to-date inspection sticker."

The site inspector shrugged. "We don't have an industrial sideloader. Never have."

"Of course, you have an industrial sideloader," the inspector argued, and pointed. "It's right there."

"That's a forklift," the site supervisor said. "Oh hell, were you talking about the forklift?"

Decipher This

Let's try our hand at writing plain language. Take this example and see what you might do with it. First, start by identifying what it is about the paragraph that will make it difficult for readers to understand the

> content clearly and easily. In essence, how does this paragraph violate the principles of plain language?
>
> Once you understand what doesn't work, take a stab at rewriting it.
>
> A "deductible" is defined as:
> Fixed amount or percentage of an insurance claim that is the responsibility of the insured, and which the insurance company will deduct from the claim payment. Sometimes deductibles are voluntary (to qualify for a lower premium rate) but usually they are imposed by the insurer to avoid paying a large number of small claims. Also called excess. Not to be confused with tax deduction.

Pièce de Résistance

Plain language simply makes sense. Audiences get content that is accessible and informative. Senders (that's us) achieve our purpose in communicating, we don't have to communicate again to clarify or correct something, and we build goodwill. Complaints go down and noise diminishes.

So why isn't everyone rushing to embrace plain language. There are several reasons. Let's start with how language is used. There are three levels. They are often given different names, but they ultimately look like this.

Formal level. This level, sometimes called the superstandard level, is bureaucratic, elevated language. Longer sentences, longer words, longer paragraphs are preferred. Repetition is welcomed. Traditionally, this level has been the language of law, medicine, and academia.

Informal level. Sometimes called the standard level of language, this is the level used in our day-to-day workplaces. It is the operational language of government and business. Simplicity and clarity are preferred because they are more efficient and effective.

Substandard level. Just as the name implies, this is communication that is unacceptable for professional messages. The word "ain't," for example, is not grammatically correct and does not convey an impression of skill and knowledge. However, "ain't" might be the perfect word for a character in a screenplay, a line of dialogue in a novel.

Over time, as demands for language that actually means something have grown, greater demand has been put on public and private organizations to use the informal level of language, the plain language equivalent. Law has largely moved to this level; so has medicine. Academia—the college essay, the academic journal article, the scholarly conference presentation—remains the last true bastion of the formal level of language.

For many new graduates, the shift from formal to informal communication can be difficult. The two-page summary comes back covered in red ink with a request to cut it in half. The expert, ensconced in jargon, technical terms, and an array of acronyms, is stymied when presentation evaluations are less rave review and more two thumbs down.

Change is hard. The shift to plain language requires us to think differently when we communicate, and we may resent or resist that requirement. We'll argue it takes more time. Indeed, it often does. But in the end, it saves us time and even frustration. We avoid miscommunication; there is no need for additional communications to clarify our original message, and we build goodwill.

The resistance movement also contends that plain language dumbs down content. It actually does the reverse. It uses a language that audiences understand and shows respect for the audience by doing this. If we think this is dumbing down, we need to think about all the things we don't know—nuclear physics, brain surgery, financial auditing, spinach cultivation—and how difficult it would be for us if we were presented with technical material in a field that isn't ours.

Try your hand at these examples from Joe Flood's *Solar Storm: A Real-World Case for Plain Language*:

> *National Oceanic and Atmospheric Administration (NOAA)*
> The latest model run now indicates the CME associated with yesterday's R3 (Strong) Radio Blackout event will impact the earth's magnetic field around 9:00 a.m. EDT (1300 UTC) on Saturday, July 14. SWPC is forecasting category G1 (Minor) Geomagnetic Storm activity then, with a chance of G2 (Moderate) levels at

times through July 15. The S1 (Minor) Solar Radiation Storm persists just above event threshold. Region 1520 has decayed in the past 12 hours, but is still potentially eruptive.

National Aeronautics and Space Administration (NASA) Based on preliminary heliospheric modeling carried out at NASA GSFC Space Weather Center, it is estimated that the CME may impact Earth, Messenger, Spitzer, MSL, Mars. Simulations indicate that the leading edge of the CME will reach Earth at about 2012-07-14T09:17Z (plus minus 7 hours). The roughly estimated expected range of the Kp maximum (Kp is a measure of geomagnetic disturbance levels ranging 0–9) is 6–8 (moderate to severe).

NOAA and NASA, Flood points out, provide two different forecasts about the looming solar storm, ominously described as "a wave of plasma stoked by an X-class solar flare."

Flood challenges anyone without a PhD in astrophysics to untangle the acronym-choked language that the two agencies use. Here's what he says he would do to convey the information:

At some point in the future—especially with the solar cycle nearing its peak—it's possible that a severe geomagnetic storm could threaten Earth with serious implications for satellite-based navigation and our power grid.

It is:

- Understandable
- Conversational
- Articulate

It is not:

- Baby talk
- Condescending
- Ineffective

WII-FM

Another related concern is that plain language will make the writer or the speaker look dumb. If we can't use the fancy words, if we can't expound at great length, people won't realize how brilliant we are. And they won't—because they stopped paying attention before we were halfway through. They left in a fog of confusion and annoyance.

There is also a belief that plain language is not necessary. People will understand what we are saying with little or no effort on their part. We know that is simply not the case. Just ask the safety inspector. Or Fairer Finance. In 2014, the research and ratings agency based in London found that of 2,000 consumers, only 27 percent said they read contract terms before accepting them. (Remember the 40-page report on your office chair.)

Of these, only 17 percent said they understood the terms.

Fast Fact

In an effort to make what they're saying to customers actually understandable, some companies are rewriting materials, including contracts. What a difference. Euroclear, a Belgium-based financial services company, rewrote its core securities contract. End result: word count was cut by 65 percent and the length went from more than 400 pages to 176, with plenty of white space.

Don't Forget the Deductible

Remember this paragraph:
A "deductible" is defined as:

Fixed amount or percentage of an insurance claim that is the responsibility of the insured, and which the insurance company will deduct from the claim payment. Sometimes deductibles are voluntary (to qualify for a lower premium rate) but usually they are imposed by the insurer to avoid paying a large number of small claims. Also called excess. Not to be confused with tax deduction.

Well Investopedia defines the term this way:

Out-of-pocket costs that you must pay before your insurance coverage kicks in and pays out your claims.

Resistance Is Futile

Regulators, governments, courts, tribunals, and others aren't waiting for organizations to move to the use of plain language. They are mandating it.

The U.S. *Affordable Healthcare Act* required that effective March 2013:

- Insurers and employers present information about insurance plans in a standardized "summary of benefits and coverage" document that describes plan features such as premiums, deductibles and co-insurance.
- Fine print literally be replaced with a minimum 12-point type size
- Cost estimates, modeled after nutrition labels on food products, must be given for three common conditions: maternity care, breast cancer, and diabetes.

In their article "Consumers' Misunderstanding of Health Insurance," George Loewenstein and coauthors note that these provisions were put in place to mitigate a widely perceived but poorly documented problem: people's lack of understanding of their health insurance. The situation is stark. In their *Journal of Health Economics* article, the authors point out that only 14 percent of respondents can correctly answer four questions about the most basic components of a health insurance plan. That doesn't mean 86 percent of people are stupid or illiterate. It means the insurance plans are unreadable.

On February 1, 2018, the Supreme Court of Canada announced that all headnotes appearing at the top of court rulings must be written in plain language and made available to the public on the court's website and Facebook pages. In a speech to law students at the University of Western Ontario in 2018, Richard Wagner, then newly appointed chief justice of the Supreme Court of Canada, said, "You have to make sure there are clear decisions accessible in clear language." It is an issue of transparency.

The Canadian Radio-Television and Telecommunications Commission (CRTC), which regulates cell phone use in Canada, has created a Wireless Code so that users of mobile wireless voice and data services will be better informed of their rights and obligations, which have often been buried or obscured in their contracts with service providers.

Here is an excerpt from the Wireless Code:

1. Plain language

A service provider must communicate with customers in a way that is clear, timely, accurate, and uses plain language.

A service provider must ensure that its written contracts and related documents, such as privacy policies and fair use policies, are written and communicated in a way that is clear and easy for customers to read and understand.

The European Union's *General Data Protection Regulation (GDPR)*, which went into effect in 2018, includes seven separate references to "clear and plain language." Here's one of them that relates to patient consent:

> The conditions for consent have been strengthened, and companies can not use long, illegible terms and conditions full of legal jargon. Under GDPR, the request for consent must be understandable and easily accessible. Consent must be clear and distinguishable from other matters and provided using clear and plain language. Additionally, GDPR states that it must be as easy to withdraw consent as it is to give it.

It's the Law

In 2010, U.S. President Barrack Obama signed into law the *Plain Writing Act*. This federal legislation:

- Requires executive agencies of government to use plain language in all communications with the general public (except regulations).

Similar laws at the state level are also in effect in several jurisdictions including California, New York, Minnesota, and Washington.

By the Numbers

In his 2017 article "To manage expectations, central banks need social media savvy," Howard Davies, chair of the Royal Bank of Scotland, notes that:

- 70 percent of the population can understand a campaign speech by Donald Trump
- 60 percent can grasp the significance of the lyrics of an Elvis Presley song
- Only 2 percent can understand the minutes of the Federal Open Market Committee
- Slightly more than 20 percent can understand what the mainstream press writes about monetary policy

Editor's Pen

Try your hand at turning this paragraph, originally from the Australia Government's Department of Finance website, "About the Department:"

As a central agency of the Australian Government, the Department of Finance (Finance) plays an important role in assisting government across a wide range of policy areas to ensure its outcomes are met. Finance supports the government's ongoing priorities through the Budget process and fosters leading practice through the public sector resource management, governance and accountability frameworks. Finance plays a lead role in advising the government on many of its strategic priorities, including advancing public sector reform through the Smaller Government Agenda and providing advice to the government on optimal arrangements for the management and ownership of public assets. We do this through our professional and considered approach to providing advice, developing policy, delivering services and engaging with our clients and stakeholders.

> Can you get this down to nine words? The department did.
> The nine words are:
> We try to help government keep to its budget.

Plain Language Pays Off

- When the U.S. Department of Veterans' Affairs rewrote a form letter to make the language plainer and clearer, the number of calls received per year plummeted from 1128 to 192.
- The U.S. Federal Communications Commission had five full-time staff members fielding calls about the rules for citizen band radios. The regulations were rewritten into plain language. Guess how many staff are needed to answer questions now. None.
- The Canadian government rewrote its Certificate to Register Livestock and compliance with the rules climbed from 40 to 95 percent.
- The Arizona Department of Revenue switched to plain language in letters to the public—and received 18,000 fewer phone calls the first year.

Main Elements of Plain Language

Frankly, there is nothing rocket science here. There is everything we have talked about up to this point—saying only what we need to say, using language audiences will understand, watching our tone—and a few other useful tips.

The most common plain language elements are as follows:

- Logical organization
- Active voice
- Common, everyday words
- Shorter words, sentences, paragraphs
- You Attitude
- Use of pronouns such as "you"

- Lists, tables, bullets
- Helpful design features such as subheads and boxes
- White space

U.S. Presidents Like Plain Language

- During his term as president, Richard Nixon announced that the Federal Register, the official daily publication for rules, proposed rules, and notices of federal agencies and organizations, must be written in "laymen's terms."
- In 1978, President Jimmy Carter issued an order about how federal regulations must be written: easy to understand and cost-effective.
- Twenty years later, President Bill Clinton declared plain language was a major government initiative and Vice President Al Gore would lead the charge.
- In 2010, President Barrack Obama signed the *Plain Writing Act of 2010* into law.

Math Makes for Easy Reading, Easy Listening

Here's a question for you. No tricks. How much is 1+1? I'm going to guess you said the answer is 2, and you are correct. Now if I ask you this question in a week, what will the answer be? In a month?

The answer, of course, remains the same regardless of when or where the question is asked. This gives numbers a sense of objectivity. There is a "right" answer and a "wrong" answer. Language is often thought of as much more subjective than numbers, figures, statistics, and data, and therefore, it is often concluded, there is no wrong way to communicate. Nothing could be further from the truth as we have discovered.

Yet the power of numbers to indicate that something is "correct" continues to convince us. So over the years, since the 1920s at least, mathematicians and linguists have been using the power of numeracy to "prove" if a piece of writing is easy to read. They have created what are called readability formulas or scores to apply a number to written text.

There are more than 200 of these formulas with names such as Robert Gunning's Fog Index; the SMOG Readability Formula; and the New Dale–Chall formula.

They all have one thing in common. Their developers looked at the complexity of language—length of words, sentences, and paragraphs—to develop a formula that would yield a number, and that number corresponds to a grade level. The higher the grade level the more difficult the piece of writing for the average reader to interpret easily and accurately.

So if a formula is applied to a paragraph and the resulting number is 13, this indicates the writing is at a first-year university level. If the number is 6, it's writing at the level grade six students could understand. A 21? Well, we'll need a few PhDs.

This raises the question of what is the optimal grade level. There is no agreed upon answer, but everyone agrees it is lower rather than higher—and it is trending downward. For several years, writing at a grade 7 or 8 level was considered plain language. This dropped to a grade six for many users, often schools, publishers, and government departments. Now many experts in the communications field are saying the best number is 5 or even 4.

That feeling on your arm and neck is a hackle. It's a common reaction to the discussion about readability formulas. Writing at a grade 6 level doesn't mean we or our audience has the intelligence, experience, or analytical ability of an 11-year-old. What it means is that our vocabulary is well formed by grade 6 (or 7 or 5), and this is the level of conversation. We're comfortable in our thongs with this language. It has nothing to do with depth or complexity of thought, analysis, or intellect. Rather, the readability score says how well we have communicated this complexity.

Let's see for ourselves. Here are some famous authors. Generally, at what grade level do you think they are writing? (This may be a range since the authors have written numerous books.)

J.K. Rowling
John Grisham
Stephen King
Jane Austen

These are authors with detailed plots, complex issues, sophisticated character development. What unites them all: we can't stop turning the page. We're engaged because we understand what they're saying, and we're drawn into the story, whether contemporary writers or from several centuries previously.

And here are the scores:

Author	Grade
J.K. Rowling	5–7
John Grisham	5–6
Stephen King	4.7
Jane Austen	7

So some of the world's most popular authors are writing at a grade 5, 6, and 7 level. Clearly they know something about great communication.

Trial Run

Here's a commonly used example to demonstrate the use of a readability score and the benefits of plain language.

Decipher This

The ideal fungicide must combine high fungitoxicity with low mammalian toxicity and phytotoxicity, and with an absence of tainting or other deleterious side effects when the fruit is processed.

Now rewrite it. Perhaps like this.

The ideal fungicide must kill fungus effectively, but must be harmless to animals and plants, and must cause no tainting or other harmful side-effects when the fruit is processed.

Now let's go a step further. We'll apply a few different readability scores to each paragraph. But before we do, what do you think the grade level will be for each paragraph?

Here are the scores. Don't worry about the name of the formula; we'll zero in on one in just a few pages. Look instead at the grade level.

Paragraph #1

The ideal fungicide must combine high fungitoxicity with low mammalian toxicity and phytotoxicity, and with an absence of tainting or other deleterious side effects when the fruit is processed.

- Flesch–Kincaid Grade Level   19.30
- Gunning–Fog Score   19.90
- Coleman–Liau Index   17.30
- SMOG Index   14.10
- Automated Readability Index   19.50

Average Grade Level   18.02

You'll notice, there are different answers depending on the formula used. Just like there are different brands of thongs and varieties of spinach, each readability formula is unique. They all agree, however, that this paragraph is difficult by any measure.

Now let's look at the revised version.

- Flesch–Kincaid Grade Level   13.80
- Gunning–Fog Score   16.00
- Coleman–Liau Index   13.10
- SMOG Index   10.10
- Automated Readability Index   16.60

Average Grade Level   13.92

The level is still high, but we have dropped four grade levels on average. That is certainly more reader friendly.

The Flesch–Kincaid Grade Level, the one we're going to talk about a little more, also has a complementary formula called a reading ease. Reading ease tells us how many people out of 100 would easily understand a piece of writing the first time they read it. So, in this case, the higher the number, the better.

Here are the reading ease scores for the two fungicidal paragraphs.

The first paragraph has a reading ease of 8.20, which means fewer than 10 percent of readers would interpret this paragraph effortlessly, thong or no thong.

The second paragraph has a reading ease of 49.50. Much improved.

In his book *How to Write Plain English* (1981, University of Canterbury), Rudolph Flesch provides this information to help us understand how reading ease relates to complexity.

Table 7.1 Flesch chart

Flesch grade level					
Estimated school grade completed	Level	Average number of words/ sentence	Average number of syllables/ word	Score	Percentage of adults who can read at this level
4th	Very easy	8 or fewer	1.23 or fewer	90–100	93
5th	Easy	11	1.31	80–90	91
6th	Fairly easy	14	1.39	70–80	88
7th or 8th	Standard	17	1.47	60–70	83
Some high school	Fairly hard	21	1.55	50–60	54
High school or some college	Hard	25	1.67	30–50	33
College	Very hard	29 or more	1.92 or more	0–30	4.5

Source: Rudolph Flesch, The Art of Readable Writing, Harper (New York).

Here's a similar chart for the Flesch-Kincaid Grade Level.

Table 7.2 Flesch Kincaid grade level

Score	School Level	Notes
100.00–90.00	5th Grade	Very easy to read. Easily understood by an average 11-year-old student
90.0–80.0	6th Grade	Easy to read. Conversational English for consumers
80.0–70.0	7th Grade	Fairly easy to read
70.0–60.0	8th to 9th Grade	Plain English. Easily understood by 13- to 15-year-old students

60.0–50.0	10th to 12th Grade	Fairly difficult to read
50.0–30.0	College	Difficult to read
30.0–0.00	College Graduate	Very difficult to read. Best understood by university graduates

Let's Zero in ...

On the Flesch Kincaid readability tests. The grade level formula was developed in 1975 and standardized by the U.S. navy beginning in 1978. The reading ease score, the 1 out of 100, was developed even earlier. The two scores go hand in hand and give us insight into the difficulty of a piece of writing.

If you're mathematically inclined, the Flesch Kincaid Grade Level formula looks like this:

206.835–1.015 (total words/total sentences)–84.6 (total syllables/total words)

Reality is most of us are never going to use this formula to calculate a readability grade level. Good news is we don't have to. Thanks to the IT whizzes at the Microsoft Corporation, every time we spell check a document, the software will provide us with a Flesch Kincaid Grade Level and reading ease score.

All you have to do is check off the box "Show readability stats." You will find it under, File, Options, Proofing.

If you turn this feature on, it will check every document for readability regardless of length, topic, or purpose.

Everything That Glitters Is Not Gold

So readability formulas have distinct advantages. They help us to understand how difficult a piece of writing may be. This understanding, in turn, gives us an opportunity to take a critical second look at our writing and make it better—for our reader (or ultimately our listener) and for achieving our purpose.

But not everything about readability formulas is rainbows and unicorns. A piece of writing may not achieve its purpose (for a number of reasons) and still get a great readability score because readability scores are looking at language not meaning. Compare these two messages.

Option 1

Susan, thanks for meeting with me today. It was very helpful. Unfortunately, the project is moving in a direction outside our areas of interest and expertise, and at this time we will step back and withdraw our participation. We wish you the best of luck.

Grade level: 6.8
Reading ease: 65.6

Option 2

Susan, what the hell! The project is off the rails. Bite me.

Grade level: 0
Reading ease: 100

Just because something is linguistically easy to read does not make it effective. Tone can still be an issue. So can comprehension. Easy to read does not mean easy to understand. Like this one.

While Olive had a spinach leaf was in the air.

Grade level: 2.4
Reading ease: 95.1

What is important to remember is that readability scores are a tool. They get us thinking about our language and whether it will work for a particular audience in a specific situation. They also point us in a direction to improve that language when needed.

That's editing, and it's coming up next.

By the Numbers

- The highest (easiest) reading ease score possible is 121.22, (i.e., every sentence contains only one-syllable words).
- "The cat sat on the mat" scores 116.
- The *Harvard Law Review* has a general readability score in the low 30s.

CHAPTER 8

Revising, Reworking, Revitalizing

Editing Essentials

Great communicators don't need an editor. They demand one. What first-rate speakers and writers alike understand is that another pair of eyes or a fresh pair of eyes are essential to successful communication. This second looks brings a new perspective, the distance that only time (even a little time) can offer, and renewed energy to improve content.

Let's try this exercise. You'll need a piece of paper, 8.5" × 11" if possible. Now transform that flat piece of paper into the world's most wonderful flying machine. The goal is to fly it as far as possible. Take a few minutes to play with different designs, then stand up and launch your creation. How far did it go?

Now let's rethink, or edit, the exercise. What did your flying machine look like? Something like this?

Let's review the instructions, the language. Nowhere did it say to build a paper airplane. It said a flying machine. The goal was distance. What would be an easier way to build a flying machine? What would get us great distance?

This would.

That's what editing does. As we write, whether for a reader or a listener, we dive in. Ideas flow. We create content. We think about our audience. We identify important points to make. We're in the midst of messaging.

When we edit, we take a step back. We come up for air. We have a different perspective and a draft on which to overlay a fresh set of eyes. Even short written messages and presentations should be edited. Think before you send or speak. Give yourself a few minutes, even just a stretch, before you hit "send" or wing it. Take one last read through or think through. You'll be surprised at what you missed or decide to revise.

Editing is essential to clear, concise, compelling communication. But editing isn't just one thing. Just as pizza isn't just one thing. There is deep dish pizza with red carnival spinach. Thin crust pepperoni and Bloomsdale spinach. New York-style pizza with Tyee spinach. Notice though that although the type of pizza is different there are common elements.

That's also true when it comes to editing. There are three broad types: substantive editing, stylistic editing, and copyediting.

Types of Editing

Substantive Editing

Substantive editing is major surgery. It involves rethinking and rewriting. This may mean revising whole paragraphs or the entire document. It may involve restructuring or reorganizing parts of the text. It may include identifying where new information is required or existing information should be deleted.

Editors Canada has this to say about substantive editing, which is also called structural or developmental editing.

Structural Editing

Assessing and shaping draft material to improve its organization and content. Changes may be suggested to or drafted for the writer. Structural editing may include:

- Revising, reordering, cutting, or expanding material
- Writing original material
- Determining whether permissions are necessary for third-party material
- Recasting material that would be better presented in another form, or revising material for a different medium (such as revising print copy for web copy)
- Clarifying plot, characterization, or thematic elements

In his PPT presentation *Making a Best Case in Your Year-End Appeal* (2009), communications expert Tom Ahern includes the following example. It's from a university looking to engage staff and faculty in its new strategic plan. The intent is to inform and motivate, maybe even excite the audience about what lies ahead. Do you think this paragraph would do that?

Original

XYZ University's strategic plan is designed to amplify the university's academic excellence. The result of a 13-month planning effort, the plan identifies strategies to enhance the university's work for students on three fronts:

- Reinterpreting the liberal arts skills of communication and critical thinking to take into account 21st-century challenges and opportunities
- Multiplying connections between students and faculty members by building on the faculty's record of original research and creativity
- Building on XYZ University's strong sense of community, locally and globally

Take a few minutes to see how you would revise this. We'll wait.

Before plunging in to start changing the language and the content, it's important to identify what needs to be improved. This is really the four-step process we talked about in Chapter 6.

So now let's deconstruct this paragraph.

XYZ University's strategic plan ... This sounds cold, like we are removed from this esteemed educational institution. It violates the You Attitude. Could easily be fixed with some copyediting by saying, "Our strategic plan," but at this point we are rethinking the paragraph. The issue that this opening few words raises is one of tone. Distancing ourselves from our readers or listeners does not engage them. Indeed, it does the opposite.

... *is designed to amplify* ... Amplify, really. When was the last time that word came up Friday night over a beer and cheese pizza with Catalina spinach?

... *the university's academic excellence.* Again with the distancing. Like our audience is not part of "the university."

The result of a 13-month planning effort ... Good, concrete information. Infuses the topic with substance. There was some work put into this plan. A bit jargony. Better to say "13 months of work," more concise and emphatic.

... *the plan identifies strategies to enhance the university's work for students on three fronts.* Again, three fronts is specific makes us want to know what those three fronts are. Interesting it is just for students, not students and faculty? Is this an oversight? Or accurate? Or is it "our work on behalf of students?"

... *Reinterpreting* ... Good grief. Warms your heart, doesn't it.

... *the liberal arts skills* ... Will readers/listeners know what this term means? If yes, great. If not, replace.

... of communication and critical thinking to take into account 21st-century challenges ... Such as? Are we not taking those challenges into account now?

... and opportunities ... Such as? Are we not taking those opportunities into account now?

... Multiplying ... And amplifying. We're on a roll.

... connections between students and faculty members by building on the faculty's record of original research and creativity ... How does this focus on faculty work build greater connections with students?

... Building on XYZ University's strong sense of community, locally and globally ... Not "our" sense of community. How will we do this? Ready for the rewrite? It will separate the thong wearers from the non-thong wearers.

Rewrite

Within a decade, if all goes according to plan, XYZ University will emerge as the top school in its class, leaving behind our "peer schools" of today. Admittedly, the plan is ambitious. And it won't be cheap: excellence in education at this level never is. But we will get there, thanks to your vision, your commitment, and your help.

Take a moment to settle in. Identify what resonated with you? What created noise? And why did it create noise?
Now, let's deconstruct.

Within a decade ... Nice. We have a time frame—a short enough timeframe that many people who are reading or hearing this may still be working at the university. Now it's starting to sound a little real, not just some dusty old document sitting on a shelf.

... if all goes according to plan ... Could be seen as a hedge, a way out if things don't work, but many people will see this as being honest. One of the likely questions people will have is about the chances of success. This isn't promising a guaranteed outcome.

XYZ University will emerge ... Still that distance but we're putting the university on a pedestal now. "Emerge" is a strong word. Many people can picture something emerging.

... as the top school in its class ... Wow, that's ambitious. We might have doubts. We might also be proud, or excited.

... leaving behind our "peer schools" of today ... That hit our competitive streak. Who doesn't want to top the leader board? Not sure why "peer schools" is in quotes or if this is a term audiences will know instantly.

... Admittedly ... Makes us sound human. Conversational.

... the plan is ambitious ... Why include this? Because readers and listeners are thinking it. Let's own it.

... And it won't be cheap. Why include this? Same reason as above. If we think about our audience, one of their key questions will be "How much is this going to cost." Let's be upfront with them. The word "cheap" may be too conversational for some. It may not sound "professional," but it does sound forthright.

... excellence in education at this level never is. What you're feeling is pride. Go team go!

... But we will get there ... Motivational

... thanks to your vision, your commitment, and your help. Great repetition of "your." It draws the audience directly into the con-

tent and makes them feel part of the plan. Reader consideration. But it needs to be sincere.

In a Nutshell

The rewrite changes tone. It pulls on our heartstrings. It uses emotion to engage. The original just bored us. And confused us. It sounded like the same old, same old.

Yawn.

Polishing Prose

Copyediting is like minor surgery. The impact can be significant, but structural changes and in-depth revisions are not necessary (or have already been done). This type of editing, the most common for most of what we write and write to present, involves editing a document for style, flow, and clarity. It also requires ensuring a consistent tone and pacing.

Editors Canada offers the following overview for stylistic editing, or line editing. Many nonprofessionals would consider this copyediting. Ultimately, it doesn't matter what we call it as long as we do it.

Stylistic Editing

Editing to clarify meaning, ensure coherence and flow, and refine the language. It includes:

- Eliminating jargon, clichés, and euphemisms
- Establishing or maintaining the language level appropriate for the intended audience, medium, and purpose
- Adjusting the length and structure of sentences and paragraphs
- Establishing or maintaining tone, mood, style, and authorial voice or level of formality

Take a stab at improving the paragraph below. It's the opening paragraph of a profile that will appear in a hospital foundation newsletter. In this case, the profile is that of a researcher doing ground-breaking work to help unconscious patients and their families. Readers will be donors, government, supporters, staff, and volunteers.

Original

> What must it be like to be in a coma, hearing and even understanding what is said to you but with no ability to communicate—not even by blinking your eyes? One such patient was set free thanks to the research of Dalhousie University Psychology Professor Patrick Noseworthy. Instead of being condemned to hopeless-case status, life as a vegetable on a hospital bed, Dr. Noseworthy's revelation that his brain was operating meant four-and-a-half months of rehabilitation and his eventual return to a normal life able to do everything except speak.

Okay, let's break this down.

What must it be like to be in a coma ... Interesting approach to engage the audience but too general to have much of an impact. Also, awkward phrasing.

... hearing and even understanding what is said to you but with no ability to communicate ... Starting to build a picture, which is effective, but wordy.
... not even by blinking your eyes? Nice imagery. We can see this. Drives home the point—and to a certain extent the futility of the situation. Always better to let our reader reach the conclusion we'd like rather than telling them what that conclusion should be.

One such patient was set free ... Trying to make a segue to the main topic, which is effective, but the language is overly dramatic.

Thanks to the research of Dalhousie University Psychology Professor Patrick Noseworthy. Now we're starting to delve into the main topic.

... Instead of being condemned to hopeless case status, life as a vegetable on a hospital bed ... Dear heavens, spare us. We can't make something engaging or important or intense by using inflated language. We need to paint a picture. Facts do this; quotes can achieve the same purpose. Description works but it needs to be specific and detailed.

... Dr. Noseworthy's revelation ... This is Popeye on a fresh can of spinach.

... that his brain ... This says it was Dr. Noseworthy's brain. It was actually the patient's.

... was operating meant four-and-a-half months ... Precise, but unnecessarily so. It interferes with the flow of the language, and it is a point that is not critical.

... of rehabilitation and his eventual return to a normal life ... Normal life is subjective and limiting. Let's change the language.

... able to do everything except speak. Again, accurate but six words for a minor point. Remember the focus is on Dr. Noseworthy. Although we distinguish between types of editing, each has its own purpose and focus, there is often overlap. This is one of those paragraphs. It's a little bit of substantive editing and stylistic editing together.

Let's go a little deeper here. Edit these phrases so they are tighter and sharper. And for every change you make, explain why you made that change in four words or less.

Original

1. ...with no ability to communicate ...
2. What must it be like to be in a coma ...
3. ... which led to the patient ...

4. ...meant four-and-a-half months of rehabilitation ...
5. ...to a normal life able to do everything except ...

Revised

1. ... unable to communicate ... *Shorter, better flow.*
2. What must it be like to be trapped in a coma ... *One word added for greater impact.*
3. ...this discovery led to the patient ... *More powerful word included.*
4. ...meant almost five months of rehabilitation ... *Or* ... meant 150 days of rehabilitation ... *Shorter, Better Flow.*
5. ... a relatively normal life ... *Shorter, Better Flow.*

What's a Copyeditor To Do

Here are six areas of focus to help ensure your document and the presentation it is based on resonates with your audience and achieves your purpose.

Check for:

Clarity

- Long sentences
- Big words
- Uncommon words
- Meaning can't be misunderstood
- Tone
- Readability

Transitions

- Between sentences
- Between paragraphs
- Movement in time, place, subject
- Usually short transition words like "however," "so," "then"

Concreteness

- Facts and figures
- Specific language
- Action verbs
- Active voice

Repetitiveness

- Ideas
- Words
- Summaries

Completeness

- 5Ws and how
- Emphasis on why
- Unanswered questions

Flow

- Logical
- Smooth
- Read out loud

Checking It Twice

Copyediting is like cosmetic surgery. After all, we want to look our best. Many of us think of this stage—and each level of editing is a stage in its own right—as proofreading. It's often what we think of as editing, that final read through to look for misplaced commas and more, but it is not editing in the sense of revising language and content to any significant extent.

According to Editors Canada, copyediting looks like this:

Copyediting

Editing to ensure correctness, accuracy, consistency, and completeness. It includes:

- Editing for grammar, spelling, punctuation, and usage
- Checking for consistency and continuity of mechanics and facts, including anachronisms, character names, and relationships
- Editing tables, figures, and lists
- Notifying designers of any unusual production requirements
- Developing a style sheet or following one that is provided
- Correcting or querying general information that should be checked for accuracy

Case Study

The Plain Language Action and Information Network (PLAIN) website includes this news release announcing that the Veteran's Benefits Administration (VBA), part of the Department of Veterans Affairs, had won the No Gobbledygook Award for 1999. Here is an example of why the department took top honors.

Original

The proceeds of your life insurance policy will be paid to your last named beneficiary of record with the Department of Veterans Affairs according to the payment option selected by you. Our experience shows that many insureds fail to keep their designations up-to-date when there are changes in their personal circumstances ... Therefore, if you desire, but have not selected the lump sum settlement option or cannot remember the option you selected, or believe your beneficiary designation is not otherwise current, we suggest you complete the enclosed form and return it to us.

Revised

We are updating our computer systems for the year 2000. This also allows us to update the way we store our records and process our claims. This is a perfect opportunity for you to update your records as well. This letter will explain what we have done to update our records and what you can do to update yours.

> *According to PLAIN*
>
> The rewritten letter [which is not shown] significantly simplifies the message in language and format. VBA presents the information in its written letter in questions and answers and provides very direct and simply stated answers compared with the "before" version, which is very vague in its purpose. The language is directed to the second person making a better connection with the intended audience of the letter. VBA uses questions and answers to:
>
> - Clearly organize the information in the letter
> - Make it easier for the recipient to understand
> - Tell how addressees can get help if they need it
>
> The analysis is not subjective. PLAIN provided the following data to show how plain language pays off.
>
> *Tracking Savings*
>
> Claims adjusters spend at least 30 minutes a claim trying to locate beneficiaries to pay claims. The average cost of locating these beneficiaries and paying their claims is $10.25 per claim. If beneficiaries respond to this letter, it will take only 9 minutes to pay the claim, at an average cost of $1.57 per claim. If policyholders respond to the letter as they did in the test mailing, the savings will be approximately $1.5 million for just those policyholders with beneficiary forms over 40 years.
>
> VBA is the first agency to track savings from plain language. The plain language rewrite of this letter resulted in a 75% increase in the number of responses to an initial test mailing of 2500 letters, compared to responses to the original letter. VBA projects that it will save over $8 million because of this rewrite, due to decreased costs of tracking down beneficiaries in order to pay claims.

As Your Own Editor ...

You need to see the big picture.

    You need to be in the weeds.

Once you've ensured that the content is complete, relevant, and flows well, take a close look at your language. Go beyond individual paragraphs and sentences to words. Surprise your audience. Draw them in. Help them to understand. Encourage them to remember.

Like this. Here are the opening lyrics for *We Are Young*, a great song by the band Fun. Complete the last line:

Give me a second I

I need to get my story straight

My friends are in the bathroom getting higher than …

The typical expression would be "higher than a kite." Fortunately, there is nothing typical about Fun.

Give me a second I

I need to get my story straight

My friends are in the bathroom getting higher than the Empire State

And now we're intrigued, impressed, and following their every word. This is what great communication does.

This is the Thong Principle.

CHAPTER 9

Proofredding

It's impotent

Let's take a few minutes to look at the forth and final stage in the writing process. (Did you catch the error?) We've already discussed preparing to communicate, drafting our thoughts and ideas, then rewriting and revising what we've written whether it is an e-mail message, a letter, a speech, or a presentation.

Now we're tired, we're ready to move on to the next task, and we're already thinking ahead to a spinach salad for lunch. But in comes a nagging little thought: Is the document really final? Does it need one more read through?

The answer is always, "Yes." If it's a three-sentence email, the final proofing will take us 30 seconds. If it's a 30-minute presentation with slides and handouts, we should order lunch in. There is a feeling, the hungrier, busier, and more tired we are, that this last step could be safely omitted. Again, we'd be wrong. Here's why.

Proofreading plays two important roles. It helps us avoid miscommunication. It helps us avoid embarrassment.

When You Can't Blame Autocorrect

Proofreading is focused on ensuring proper grammar and correct spelling as well as accuracy of language and content. Many of us will shrug this off as unimportant or irrelevant, or already accomplished in an earlier stage. Smart organizations and savvy communicators know better. Just ask the National Aeronautics and Space Administration (NASA).

In 1962, the U.S. space agency launched the Mariner 1 spacecraft to collect data on the planet Venus. Mariner 1 never made it; 293 seconds after it left the ground the spaceship was blown up. According to an official report released by the Mariner 1 Post-Flight Review Board an omitted hyphen in a line of computer code was the culprit that sent

Mariner 1 spiraling off course. Other sources say the error was caused by a missing overbar, a line that appears above text. Some say the culprit was a decimal. It doesn't matter. What matters is that the error was overlooked.

The slip-up, says British science fiction writer Arthur C. Clarke, is "the most expensive hyphen in history." When the Mariner 1 went up in flames so did $18.5 million dollars ($156 million in today's dollars).

NASA is not alone in making the annals of proofreading blunders. Lockheed Martin, the third largest aerospace company, lost $70 million in 1999 thanks to an errant comma that incorrectly tied sales price to inflation rate. The client insisted the contract be honored.

More than a decade after Lockheed Martin was licking its financial wounds, an executive at the Chilean mint signed off on the production of 1.5 million coins. Unfortunately, the pesos in question—still in circulation today—spelled the country's name wrong: CHIIE. The executive, ahem, is no longer employed at the mint.

Even when a proofreading error is unlikely to affect the bottom line significantly, it can still affect comprehension. It can send messages we didn't intend or messages that cannot be interpreted correctly.

I recently removed this from one of my favorite diners, with apologies and a generous tip. A group of us have been having brunch on Saturday mornings for years. Here's what one menu item offered up:

> Choose between three full strips of bacon, a full slice of ham or three breakfast sausage links. Each platter is served with two eggs, seasoned hashbrowns or baked beans and toast.

Okay, so without a comma after "ham" in the first sentence, we can still easily and correctly understand that we are being given a choice of three meats: bacon, ham, or sausage. However, without a comma in the second sentence there is no way we can know whether we are getting

> two eggs, a choice of seasoned hashbrowns or baked beans, and toast
> or
> two eggs, seasoned hashbrowns, and a choice of baked beans or toast.

Now we can guess at which option is correct (toast usually comes with breakfast), but when we force our audiences to guess, we run the risk they will guess incorrectly. As effective communicators, we want to take the guesswork out of everything we have to say.

Saying Face

As we've seen, proofreading errors can be costly. Even without large price tags, overlooked grammar, punctuation, spelling, and related errors often require repeat communication and explanation. A waste of time for everyone.

Such errors are also potentially embarrassing. They can affect our credibility and reputation. They can raise questions about our competence and the care we bring to our work.

One of the all-time proofreading bloopers dates back to 1631 when royal printers in London were preparing a bible—and left out an important word in one of the 10 commandments. In that unfortunate version of the bible, sometimes called the Wicked Bible, a new decree can be found: Thou shalt commit adultery.

Then there was the 2012 University of Texas at Austin commencement program that noted on the cover the event would take place at the Lyndon B. Johnson School of Pubic Affairs. Oh dear. (This error is not as uncommon as we'd think, but it is always regrettable and always embarrassing.)

In 2008, a New Hampshire newspaper misspelled its own name as the *Valley Newss*. Now how much confidence does that give us in the quality of the reporting. To the paper's credit, the editor ran this apologetic note:

> Readers may have noticed that the *Valley News* misspelled its own name on yesterday's front page. Given that we routinely call on other institutions to hold themselves accountable for their mistakes, let us say for the record: We sure feel silly.

It's a feeling most of us would like to avoid, especially when we are building and maintaining reputations as reliable, skilled professionals. The good news is proofreading can help us here.

That's Not Yesterday's News

There is a widespread belief that small language and grammar errors don't matter today. We're using technology in new and evolving ways, and grammar has gone by the wayside. Texting, emojis, even e-mail have given us a new set of rules, and it's only old folks who eat spinach that contend otherwise.

Actually, it's our readers, our listeners, and our employers who contend otherwise. A study conducted by the College Board, established through the National Commission on Writing to improve writing and learning in American schools, found 50 percent of the organizations that responded look at writing skill when hiring professional staff. In addition, at least 80 percent of the companies in the service and finance, insurance, and real estate sectors, those corporations with the greatest employment growth potential, assess writing during hiring. This is a critical skill, and proofreading errors raise red flags about our capability.

Test Your Skills

Take a look at the following sentence. How many Fs are there?

> Finished files are the result of years of scientific study combined with the experience of years.

If you said, six, you're correct. If you said, three or five, you've hit on the two reasons why proofreading can be so difficult.

Many people miss the three "Fs" in "of." Small words like these are often overlooked as we read through a slide or other piece of text. Our brain understands what should be there, and we see what we expect to see. We glide over the small words and believe them to be correct.

The other often-missed "F" is in the final "of." This is an issue of speed and tiredness. Proofreading requires attention and focus. It's not unusual to rush the process or find ourselves getting tired and distracted—even when it's only one sentence. That's one reason so many PPTX slides and short e-mails have errors. Inevitably, those errors are noticed by our audience.

Slowing Down Your Eyes

One reason we miss mistakes is because our eyes are moving at breakneck speed. The brain, in turn, rushes to keep pace. The result: the "l" is dropped in public or we dine on kinfolk. (Keep reading.) Many proofreading techniques, therefore, are intended to slow our eyes down. Here are a few:

1. If proofreading a paper version (often recommended as well to give eyes and brain a break from the same-old, same-old), use a finger or a pencil to go through the material word by word. Remember, at this stage we are not reading for content and comprehension, so it doesn't matter if the flow is affected. (We can also do this with text on the screen.)
2. Read from the bottom up.
3. Read one line—not one sentence—at a time. Using a ruler or a piece of paper to hide the other text will help here.
4. Proofread for specific items. For example, if there is a word, title, or name that is commonly misspelled, have spell check look for incorrect variations of this word or search for the first few letters. This technique also gives your brain a rest.
5. Fact check separately from proofreading. Part of proofreading is making sure content is correct. This is fact checking. Confirm that phone numbers and website links actually work. Check the title of documents cited and the names of people mentioned.
6. Read the text aloud and word for word. (If the text is for a presentation, read what is on the slide not what will be said when the slide appears.)
7. Pay special attention to titles, subheads, footnotes, and other material that isn't part of the main blocks of text. This is where errors occur. Just ask the *Valley News*.
8. Try reading on an incline. It's actually much less tiring on the body.

Giving Your Brain a Break

Proofreading should be done separately from editing. So give yourself a break—and a fresh set of eyes—before tackling this final step. Here's how.

1. If the text is short, stand up, breathe deep, maybe do a stretch. Then proofread.
2. Proofread differently from *how* you write and/or edit. For most of us, this is sitting in front of a computer screen. So print material and proofread on paper.
3. Proofread differently from *where* you write and edit. Is a boardroom available? A meeting room? A favorite and quiet coffee shop? This new environment will help position material in a new way. Your brain feels like this is not drudgery.
4. Get rid of distractions. Turn the phone off (or leave it in the office). Move away from mainstream traffic in the workplace.
5. After an hour, stop. Take a walk, go for lunch and indulge in a spinach-artichoke dip. Take your thong to the cleaner. Come back refreshed.
6. Ask another person to proofread the work. This needs to be someone who will read with care and not get caught up in content.

In Fine Style

For those who do a lot of writing, oversee employees who do a lot of writing, and/or write long documents, creating an in-house style guide may be useful. First, select a grammar book that will be the default reference for answering questions about everything from commas to capitalization to compound sentences. One of the best-selling and highly recommended is *The Chicago Manual of Style*.

But any grammar book will give only the rules and how those rules are put into practice, or not. It may not answer questions specific to your issue or your industry. That's where a style guide comes in.

A style guide is tailor-made for a specific company, department, or topic. It details how words will be spelled, titles capitalized, acceptable abbreviations, exceptions to common usage, and more. We recently proofread an annual report for an airport authority, which oversees operation of an international airport. The style guide we developed, for example, noted that "under way" is how the organization spells the use of the term in phrases like, "The project is under way." The word "underway" spelled as one word, however, refers specifically, and more rarely, to activities such as underway refueling.

Now, we'll get under way discussing the importance of feedback.

> ### You May Have Seen This T-Shirt
> *Let's eat Grandma.*
> *Let's eat, Grandma.*
> Proofreading can save the life of someone you love.

CHAPTER 10

To Give and Receive

The feedback loop

We talked earlier about the basic communications process. It looks like this:

Sender → Message → Medium → Receiver

There is another—and important—element in this process:

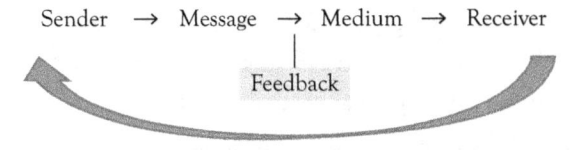

Speakers get instant feedback. We can look at the expressions on listeners' faces; we can read their body language. Are they smiling? Yawning? Arms crossed? These are important signals about how our message is being received and if we are connecting with our audience, regardless of its size.

Indeed, gestures and body language are the main factor used by people to interpret a message. As we said earlier, they account for 55 percent of the meaning we derive. Words account for only 7 percent.

As speakers, we can instantly adjust our message, our tone, our approach, and our body language based on the implicit and explicit feedback we get from listeners. As writers, there will be a delay in getting that feedback, and sometimes we get no response at all, which can be difficult to decipher.

Feedback is critical for two reasons. First, it lets us adjust our content and tone immediately or relatively quickly in the case of some written messages like e-mails. Second, it enables us to further hone our skills, to determine what works well and what doesn't. So as good, even great, communicators we seek out feedback.

Many people would rather have an enema. There's something about feedback that makes many of us cringe, and we get feelings of dread. Similar to eating kale. But giving or receiving feedback doesn't have to be ferocious—or feared. In fact, it shouldn't be.

Feedback Without Fear

Let's put the topic in context. For our purposes, feedback is information about our communication—content and tone—that will help us become better writers and speakers. We also give feedback to help people understand what they do well and how they could do better. Feedback is not about showing superiority. It is not about glossing over or ignoring issues. It's not about telling people they did a great job when they didn't, and it's not about seeking out a glowing review of our communications skills. It's about identifying what we could do better.

And this, frankly, can scare the spinach out of us. It is about wearing a thong with confidence. That said, it is important to understand why giving and receiving feedback intimidates many of us.

Giving feedback is difficult both personally and professionally. As a boss, a colleague, a partner, we don't want to hurt anyone's feelings—and we don't want to be perceived as being mean. We want to be liked, and we worry saying something "not nice," at the very least not positive, will alter people's views of us. This concern is also tied to another feedback reality: what's the best way to do this?

As receivers of feedback—criticism really—we feel vulnerable. We don't want to be told we're not perfect, even though we suspect this may be the case. It's hard to stand before someone, literally or figuratively, and expose ourselves warts and all. We'd rather be told we're doing a great job and leave it at that. Critiques can be hard to handle objectively. There is a tendency to take things personally, to let the noise consume our thoughts.

There's a Charles Schulz Peanuts cartoon where Lucy yells at the back of a retreating Linus, "You can't take destructive criticism." And therein lies the aversion to feedback: it can be hurtful, whether intentionally or otherwise.

So, let's look at feedback in a new light: it's not about personal failure and it's not about being a miserable human being. It's about helping ourselves and others to communicate better. When that happens, everyone benefits.

Types of Feedback

We've been talking about feedback as if it is one thing. In their book *Thanks for the Feedback: The Science and Art of Receiving Feedback Well*, Douglas Stone and Sheila Heen point out that feedback falls into three groups.

First, there is appreciation. This is about more than saying thank you. It's about connecting with another person in a fundamental way. It's also about demonstrating that an individual has value—and we see that value.

Coaching is another type of feedback. The emphasis here is on growth and development, and finding collective solutions that will help someone improve their skills.

Finally, there is evaluation. This is typically exemplified by the quarterly or annual performance review. Indeed, many organizations actually use an assessment checklist as a means of providing feedback. Stone and Heen note that this type of feedback aligns expectations, clarifies consequences, and informs decision making. It also compares an individual to other individuals, a set of standards, or other performance measures.

Understanding that feedback is not one thing serves as a critical reminder that whether we are giving or receiving feedback, we need to set goals. What is it we are trying to achieve? How will we know if we have achieved the desired outcomes? How do we want to feel about giving/receiving feedback? How do we want the other person (or people) to feel?

Give Pause

If we're asking for feedback, either formal or informal, we need to be open and receptive to the comments we get back. That means preparing ourselves to hear that, surprisingly, we're not perfect. There will be room for improvement. However, if we take those comments in the spirit in which they were intended, we will actually appreciate the feedback and put it to use. As our thin skin gets thicker and we become more open to hearing how we could improve, we can reach out to those whose feedback we might most dread: bosses, friends, close colleagues.

When we are the feedback givers, we need to consider our listener or reader. It's important to have a clear understanding of what they want from us. If they're asking for comments on a report, there is no need to discuss their, admittedly dreadful, presentation skills. When giving feedback face to face or over the phone, we have a greater opportunity to understand how our comments are being received. Is the body language receptive? Does the tone of voice sound tense? Relaxed? Do facial expressions convey openness with a hint of a grin or is it more like a deer in the headlights? We'll adjust accordingly.

Keeping our feedback as descriptive, direct, and clear as possible is critical. If we're on the receiving end, we'll be sure to request this by, for instance, asking, "Could you give me an example?" "Would you mind explaining that in a little more detail?" "Would it be helpful if I did X?"

Personally Speaking

One of the main causes of noise is moving from the professional (the objective) to the personal (the subjective). Once listeners and readers start taking things personally, they will react emotionally and, often, negatively. They may get defensive; they may get upset; they may get angry. What they don't get is our message.

To stay out of emotional quicksand, focus on the person's behavior, skills, or performance and not the person themselves. This is more neutral ground. The content must also be relevant. If we're talking about why spinach crop yields are down, there is no need to bring up kale. Or Bluto. Equally important: stay away from comparisons, especially to other people.

Tone is paramount here. We must sound nonjudgmental, whether we're speaking or writing. It's back to neutral territory—but supportive neutral territory. The "proof" of our four-step process helps here. It documents that we are not lashing out, trying to mark our territory, or getting even. It's about constructive, not destructive, criticism.

One way to demonstrate support and professionalism is to offer solutions, when possible. Frankly, it's easy to enumerate another person's shortcomings. It's much harder—and far more productive—to help them effectively address issues. Remember the company in Chapter 2 that received a request from a charity to post a sign in their parking lot. The company had to turn that request down. How much more sincere would the company have sounded and how much goodwill would they have built if a solution had been offered. Like this:

> I have spoken with Bill Barnacle, owner of the Farmers' Market on the corner of Central and Second Street. He would be pleased to post a sign for you in his parking lot. Bill can be reached at 555-SPINACH.

Now imagine the reaction from the reader when they read this paragraph. That's what offering solutions does; it takes the sting away from the negative news and it builds goodwill.

Solutions, however, should be offered up as suggestions or opportunities and not a "fix" to a problem or problems that need to be resolved. If we can provide proposed solutions while encouraging reflection, we have a greater chance that our audience will understand the feedback.

Listen Up

There is a difference between hearing and listening. Much of the time as someone is speaking, we are already formulating our response—or our objections. Active listening calls on us to do something far differently and far more effectively. It starts with us actually listening. This means we're not thinking about the spinach casserole for supper, trying to figure out what that annoying background sound is, or clenching because we're bored out of our minds.

Active listening, sometimes called reflective listening, requires us to be engaged in the conversation—as a listener. We won't sit there passively. We'll take notes, we'll lean in, we'll nod, we'll smile. We will look at the speaker.

This is feedback. It will let the speaker know we are paying attention, we are interested, we are working to understand the content.

> ### I'm Listening
>
> In an article in *Forbes* magazine, Dianne Schilling recommends the following 10 steps to effective listening. How many do you routinely use?
>
> - Face the speaker and maintain eye contact.
> - Be attentive yet relaxed.
> - Keep an open mind.
> - Listen to the words and try to picture what the speaker is saying.
> - Don't interrupt and don't impose your "solutions."
> - Wait for the speaker to pause to ask clarifying questions.
> - Ask questions only to ensure understanding of something that has been said (avoiding questions that disrupt the speaker's train of thought).
> - Try to feel what the speaker is feeling.
> - Give the speaker regular feedback (e.g., summarize, reflect feelings, or simply say "uh huh").
> - Pay attention to what isn't said—to feelings, facial expressions, gestures, posture, and other nonverbal cues.

Such feedback builds trust and goodwill. It also reduces misunderstanding and miscommunication.

Writers can also actively listen although we don't call it that. We call it paying close attention to what has been said and how it has been said. Can we understand the main points? Is the message clear? Is the tone friendly and relaxed? Stiff and formal? Then we respond.

Frankly, My Dear

In an effort to allay—or avoid—the negative emotions that can be wrapped up in giving and receiving feedback (especially when we know in advance the feedback is coming), we often default to "being nice." This makes us feel better no matter what side of the communications fence we're on. No one's feelings are hurt, there is no animosity on either side. All in all, a job well done.

Not.

When we give or get feedback that is full of platitudes and roses, we may feel good, but we've missed the mark. Feedback is about helping individuals and organizations perform better. It's about motivation and direction. Taking the easy way out simply doesn't work. It's also not appreciated.

Most people receiving feedback want to know how they can improve (at the very least they need to know); those giving the feedback need to help them understand how they can do just that. Frankness is essential. When we are open and honest about what we need and what we have to say, that openness helps to build trust and engagement. There are short-term and long-term benefits.

Frankness—being direct and sincere—is not to be confused, however, with bluntness. These are often confused. Delivering bad news or difficult news can be done in a way that builds rapport and greater understanding. This is being forthright. Delivering bad news or difficult news can also be done in a way that damages relationships and creates noise instead of insight. This is being blunt. It's often another way to say rude.

We have to avoid defending being rude or hurtful with the excuse that we are only speaking the truth or being honest. In fact, we're being mean. And meanness does not enhance communication—it prevents messages from being received and it destroys goodwill.

The Feedback Sandwich

To soften the blow of bad news, to build a rapport with our audience, and to offer positive reinforcement, it's often recommended that we create a feedback sandwich. This approach calls for wedging the negative content—the meat of the sandwich—between two positive slices of information. If we start and end on a positive note, our listener or reader will be more likely to get the message and appreciate us for it.

That's not always the case. Some experts contend it's rarely the case. One of the drawbacks to the feedback sandwich is that the positive reinforcement gets lost in the organization of information. It's important to understand how the audience will react. While the positive opening pumps us up, this good feeling flies right out the door as soon as the negative comments start rolling in.

Then comes the criticism, the spotlight on our flaws. We give that full attention, and we are on full alert. It's almost like we've been ambushed. Now we don't hear the nice, warm comments at the end because we're poised for another onslaught of adverse info or we're too focused on the negative feedback.

In fact, we're hardwired to focus on the negative. Clifford Nass, a professor of communication at Stanford University who wrote *The Man Who Lied to His Laptop: What Machines Teach Us About Human Relationships*, notes that most of us remember negative things more strongly and in more detail than we do positive things. There's a biological reason for this.

To process negative emotions, we need to spend more time thinking. As a result, information is more fully processed. We also tend to use more powerful words to describe negative emotions, words that are more easily stored in our brain and recalled.

Feedback Pitfalls

In their 2017 article "How to give and receive feedback effectively," Georgia Hardavella et al. identify nine barriers to effective feedback. They are:

1. Generalized feedback not related to specific facts
2. Lack of advice on how to improve behavior
3. A lack of respect for the source of feedback
4. Fear of upsetting colleagues

> 5. Fear of damaging professional relationships
> 6. Defensive behavior/resistance when receiving feedback
> 7. Physical barriers: noise, or improper time, place or space
> 8. Personal agendas
> 9. Lack of confidence

Feedback Mechanism

Another reason the feedback sandwich fails to work is that audiences are overly familiar with the technique. It is often the default process for performance reviews. So, we don't hear the good stuff because we're waiting for the bad news. Then that's all we can focus on.

Let's try serving up a different model. Let's start with the negative. Dive in and hoist up a few treasures from the ocean depths. These must be important finds, and ideally, issues with options for improvement that can be discussed. Guess what follows the few, albeit significant, negative points? A long, relevant and sincere list of positive information.

Audiences will sigh with relief. And smile. They won't even have to adjust their thong.

About the Author

donalee Moulton is a professional wordsmith. She is a communications specialist, award-winning writer, and freelance journalist with more than 25 years of experience.

donalee is the owner of Quantum Communications, a communications company based in Halifax, Nova Scotia. As a consultant, donalee has provided clients across Canada, the United States, and beyond with a wide range of services, including comprehensive editorial services, media relations, government relations, business planning, and communications planning. As a professional writer and editor, donalee has prepared everything from brochures to booklets, newsletters to annual reports, websites to online content, marketing kits to feature articles, manuals to users' guides.

As well, donalee is a professional educator and trainer. She has taught business communication at Dalhousie University and Saint Mary's University and public relations and communications courses at Mount Saint Vincent University.

In addition to her communications and training work, donalee is a professional journalist. Her byline has appeared in more than 100 magazines and newspapers including *The National Post*, *Investment Executive*, *The Lawyers Daily*, *The Medical Post*, *Chatelaine*, and *The Globe & Mail*. She is a coauthor of the book *Celebrity Court Cases: Trials of the Rich and Famous*.

For donalee, communicating effectively is about much more than finding the right word. It's about understanding your audience and tailoring a message to meet their needs—and ultimately yours. That's why, for example, she recommends not starting cover letters with "Yo Dawg." donalee also believes that learning should be filled with laughter.

Index

action verbs, 44
active listening, 117, 118
Affordable Healthcare Act, 80
ambiguous language, 40
audience, 63, 66–67

Barnum, P. T., 2–3
body language, 50, 113, 116

Canadian Radio-Television and Telecommunications Commission (CRTC), 80–81
Catcher in the Rye, The (Salinger), 38–39
center stage, 36
Chicago Manual of Style, The, 110
clarity, 7–10, 22, 35, 55, 56, 59, 76, 97, 100
coaching, 115
communications, 6, 18, 29, 33–36, 38, 39, 49, 50, 57–62, 69, 77, 113, 114
completeness, 101
conciseness, 17–18, 22, 28, 30, 35, 53, 69
concrete language, 43, 55, 64
concreteness, 101
consideration, 36, 56, 97
copyediting, 97, 101–102
copyeditor, 100–101
credibility, 57
Cycle to Civility, 53

dastardly language, 40–41
Davies, H., 82
deductible, 76, 79
Department of Finance (Finance), 82
distractions and gnats, 34–35
double entendre, 39–40

editing, 91–92
  nutshell, 97
  original, 93–95
  rewrite, 95–97
  structural, 93
  substantive, 92
elevated language, 1, 4, 9, 43–44
Euroclear, 79

feedback, 113–114
  fear and, 114–115
  loop, 113
  mechanism, 121
  sandwich, 119–120
  types of, 115
Flesch chart, 88
Flesch Kincaid grade level, 87–89
Flesch, R., 88
flow, 101
formal level, 76
four-step process, 61–68
frankness, 119

General Data Protection Regulation (GDPR), 81
gestures, 50, 113
goodwill, 57–62, 64, 68–70, 73

human connection, 49–51

informal level, 76
inner circle, 51–53

key messages, 63–64, 67

lexical ambiguity, 38
linking verbs, 44
listening, 117–118
lucidity, 12–13

Making a Best Case in Your Year-End Appeal (2009), 93
medium, 33, 93, 97, 113
Mehrabian, A., 49–50
message, 33–39, 47–53, 113
miscommunication, 1, 2, 38, 39, 77, 105, 118

National Aeronautics and Space Administration (NASA), 78
National Oceanic and Atmospheric Administration (NOAA), 77–78
next-friday syndrome, 38–39
noise maker, 47–49

online writing lab (OWL), 25
original editing, 93–95
O-ring resiliency, 4

package benefits, 75
pièce de résistance, 76–78
plain language, 5, 73–81, 85, 86, 103
    elements of, 83–84
    pays off, 83
    U.S. Presidents and, 84
Plain Language Association International (PLAIN), 21, 73–74, 102, 103
Plain Writing Act, 81
poetic license, 41–42
polishing prose, 97–100
presentations, 1, 5, 14, 18–20, 24–26, 28, 35, 64, 77, 92, 105
proof, 64–65, 67–68
proofreading, 101, 105–111
purpose, 61–62, 65

readability, 22, 29, 85, 86, 89, 90
    formulas, 84, 85, 87, 89–90
    score, 85, 86, 90
reader-based prose, 36
reading ease, 87–90

receiver, 33, 34, 37, 45, 47, 53, 56, 69, 113, 114
reflective listening, 117, 118
relevance, 26–27
repetition, 24–25
repetitiveness, 101
reputation, 57
resistance, 80–81
revising, 92, 93, 101, 105
rewrite, 95–97
rude, 53

Salinger, J. D., 38–39
sender, 33, 34, 38, 43, 47, 53, 69, 76, 113
Silent Messages (Mehrabian), 49–50
spinach, 7, 22–24, 28, 36, 38, 41, 64, 66, 92, 105, 108, 114, 116, 117
structural editing, 93
stylistic editing, 97–100
substandard level, 76–77
substantive editing, 92

thong, 41, 59, 62, 69, 85, 87, 88, 95, 110, 114, 121
Thong Principle, 59, 69, 70, 104
tone, 4, 9, 17, 47–53, 55–57, 59–61, 63, 66, 83, 90, 94, 97, 113, 114, 117
transitions, 100
trust, 1, 4, 6, 42, 47, 57–59, 73, 118, 119
truth, 38, 39, 60, 84, 119

verbs, 44
Veteran Benefits Administration (VBA), 102, 103

WII-FM, 79
written communications, 1

You Attitude, 8, 36, 38, 49, 52, 94

OTHER TITLES IN THE CORPORATE COMMUNICATION COLLECTION

Debbie DuFrene, Stephen F. Austin State University, Editor

- *101 Tips for Improving Your Business Communication* by Edward Barr
- *Business Writing For Innovators and Change-Makers* by Dawn Henwood
- *Delivering Effective Virtual Presentations* by Virginia K. Hemby
- *New Insights into Prognostic Data Analytics in Corporate Communication* by Pragyan Rath and Kumari Shalini
- *Leadership Through A Screen* by Joseph Brady and Garry Prentice
- *Managerial Communication for Professional Development* by Reginald L. Bell and Jeanette S. Martin
- *Managerial Communication for Organizational Development* by Reginald L. Bell and Jeanette S. Martin
- *Business Report Guides* by Dorinda Clippinger
- *Strategic Thinking and Writing* by Michael Edmondson
- *Conducting Business Across Borders* by Adrian Wallwork
- *English Business Jargon and Slang* by St. Suzan Maur
- *Business Research Reporting* by Dorinda Clippinger
- *64 Surefire Strategies for Being Understood When Communicating with Co-Workers* by St. Walter John
- *Communicating to Lead and Motivate* by William C. Sharbrough
- *Managerial Communication and the Brain* by Dirk Remley

Concise and Applied Business Books

The Collection listed above is one of 30 business subject collections that Business Expert Press has grown to make BEP a premiere publisher of print and digital books. Our concise and applied books are for...

- Professionals and Practitioners
- Faculty who adopt our books for courses
- Librarians who know that BEP's Digital Libraries are a unique way to offer students ebooks to download, not restricted with any digital rights management
- Executive Training Course Leaders
- Business Seminar Organizers

Business Expert Press books are for anyone who needs to dig deeper on business ideas, goals, and solutions to everyday problems. Whether one print book, one ebook, or buying a digital library of 110 ebooks, we remain the affordable and smart way to be business smart. For more information, please visit www.businessexpertpress.com, or contact sales@businessexpertpress.com.

www.ingramcontent.com/pod-product-compliance
Lightning Source LLC
Chambersburg PA
CBHW051751230426
43670CB00012B/2246